PENG

FAMOU

Over fifty years have passed si_____ ___ ____g___
Famous Trials appeared. This reissue of nine volumes of the famous series covering notorious crimes and trials from the mid nineteenth century onwards remains true to the original text and just as fascinating to modern readers.

The Penguin *Famous Trials* series has its origins in *The Notable British Trials Series* which was founded in 1905 by Harry Hodge. As Managing Director of William Hodge & Co. Ltd, Publishers and Shorthand Writers, Hodge had a vast knowledge of both the Scottish Courts and criminology – he was himself an expert short-hand writer and this is reflected in his careful selection of editors and his insistence on accurate reporting of trials for *The Notable British Trials Series*. As the original editor of the Penguin *Famous Trials* (Volumes 1 and 2), Hodge chose the most intriguing crimes, remaining firm to his belief that a crime should be at least twenty years old before it can prove itself 'notable'. After his death in 1947 his son, James Hozier Hodge, went on to become general editor of the Penguin *Famous Trials* series.

FAMOUS TRIALS 2

————————

Herbert Rowse Armstrong
Field and Gray
George Joseph Smith
Ronald True

EDITED BY HARRY HODGE

PENGUIN BOOKS

PENGUIN BOOKS

Published by the Penguin Group
Penguin Books Ltd, 27 Wrights Lane, London W8 5TZ, England
Penguin Books USA Inc., 375 Hudson Street, New York, New York 10014, USA
Penguin Books Australia Ltd, Ringwood, Victoria, Australia
Penguin Books Canada Ltd, 10 Alcorn Avenue, Toronto, Ontario, Canada M4V 3B2
Penguin Books (NZ) Ltd, 182–190 Wairau Road, Auckland 10, New Zealand

Penguin Books Ltd, Registered Offices: Harmondsworth, Middlesex, England

First published 1948
3 5 7 9 10 8 6 4 2

Copyright 1948 by William Hodge & Co (Holdings) Ltd
All rights reserved

Printed in England by Clays Ltd, St Ives plc

PREFACE

"Has a murder been committed? Who ever beheld the ghastly corpse of the murdered innocent weltering in its blood and did not feel his own blood run cold and slow through all his veins? Has the murderer escaped? With what eagerness do we pursue? With what zeal do we apprehend? With what joy do we bring to justice? And when the dreadful sentence of death is pronounced upon him, everybody hears it with satisfaction, and acknowledges the justice of the divine denunciation that, 'By whom man's blood is shed, by man shall his blood be shed.'"

These words, spoken by the Prosecuting Counsel at the trial of Mary Blandy in 1752, evoke an answering thrill even to-day. Crime—especially murder—holds a perennial appeal. If we are prevented from being present at the actual hearing, the evidence, in cold print, the speeches for and against the accused, even the photographs of the locus or grisly relics produced in Court, can all make a criminal trial a thing of flesh-and-blood and grim actuality. Here is a quartette of cases, famous in their day, which bring alive again the four men who paid the penalty for their hateful deeds. The fifth still exists in Broadmoor.

Field and Gray, who slew a girl of seventeen on a lonely beach at Eastbourne for the trivial sum her purse contained, were undesirable products of the first World War, unemployed, pleasure-loving, stupid and brutal. Herbert Rowse Armstrong, borrowing his methods from the acquitted Harold Greenwood, is a curious study in the conceited criminal mentality, a secret poisoner who committed one murder and might never have been suspected as his wife's slayer but for his clumsy attempt to destroy a rival solicitor by the same means. Ronald True, whose case bears odiously similar features to the recent trial of Heath, was, like the latter, an abnormal personality, later adjudged insane and belatedly reprieved. George Joseph Smith will be forever associated with cheap lodgings and that article of household use indispensable to his activities—a bath.

Many years have passed since their grim dramas were staged and the curtain rung down on the last act. Mass-murder on a colossal scale has been committed to shock humanity, yet these queer, sinister, inexplicable figures still persist and appeal to those who love to probe the murderer's psychology. Dickens spoke the last word when he wrote of this: "For what could she know of the criminal intellect, which its own professed students perpetually misread, because they persist in trying to reconcile it with the average intellect of average men, instead of identifying it as a horrible wonder apart?"

HARRY HODGE

EDINBURGH

CONTENTS

HERBERT ROWSE ARMSTRONG

(1922)

By Filson Young

I

THE little town of Hay in Brecon lies pleasantly just over the Welsh border (its railway station is in England) along the right bank of the River Wye, surrounded in the near distance by such wild hills as Hay Bluff, Lord Hereford's Knob, and the Brecon Beacons. It is a sunny, quaint little place, with irregular, old-fashioned houses and a broad High Street pleasantly lending itself to gossip and the observation of other people's affairs; and behind its quiet gardens, with an endless ripple and chime, runs the river in broad and shining reaches.

II

The legal business of the town and of the farmers in the neighbouring countryside was, in the year 1906, when this story opens, conducted by two firms of solicitors (both of old standing), whose offices faced one another across the main street. The head of one firm was Mr. Cheese, and of the other Mr. Griffiths. In 1906 came Mr. Herbert Rowse Armstrong as managing clerk to Mr. Cheese. He was thirty-seven years of age, but had been admitted a solicitor in 1895, and had been in partnership and practising on his own account for over two years in Newton Abbot, his native town, as well as in Liverpool. Although of humble origin, he had been carefully educated by two maiden aunts, who, at some sacrifice, had enabled him to attend the University of Cambridge, where he graduated M.A. He had worked hard in Newton Abbot and in Liverpool, and had saved, or got, enough money to put capital into Mr. Cheese's business and to become a partner very soon after his arrival in Hay. And very soon after that Mr. Cheese and his wife both died, leaving Armstrong in sole possession of the business. A year later Armstrong married a Miss Katherine Mary Friend, and in 1907 brought her to live in a little house in the delightful coombe called Cusop Dingle, within half a mile of Hay, where many of the inhabitants have villas. Three years later he moved to a larger house a few hundred yards away called " Mayfield "—a house with a fairly large garden. During these years the three children of this marriage were born. In it they all lived until Mrs. Armstrong died, and was carried from it to Cusop Churchyard in February, 1921; and until Armstrong was arrested on the last day of the same year.

The war came and brought its changes to the lives of the people in Hay, as elsewhere. Armstrong had been a Volunteer, and had joined the Territorial branch of the Royal Engineers; and when the war came he went away and served in various parts of England. I believe he did not see any actual fighting, being chiefly engaged in depot work, where his experience as a solicitor would prove useful, and where he was still able to exercise some control over his own business. Mr. Griffiths was not so fortunate as his brother solicitor. He was getting on in years and was failing in health, and his son, who had passed his final law examination, but had not yet been admitted as a solicitor, was called away to the front. In these circumstances it became necessary for Mr. Griffiths to take a partner, and Mr. Oswald Norman Martin, who had served and been invalided out of the Army, came to join him. Mrs. Armstrong had called upon Mrs. Griffiths on hearing that a partner was coming, and had asked if her husband might not assist them. He had already made some tentative overtures on the subject of the amalgamation of the two firms, but they had not been favourably received, nor had any-

thing come of the suggestion that he should stand by until
the son could come home and take charge. After Armstrong
had been demobilized and returned to Hay, Mr. Martin was
in virtual charge of the business over the way. They met
each other, of course; everyone of a certain standing knows
everyone else in Hay; and they had professional dealings
and social associations, but they were, in a sense, rivals.
They were both, as the local people would say, foreigners,
and in matters connected with his private affairs the Welsh
farmer is not fond of employing strangers. Mr. Cheese had
been long known in the place, and so had Mr. Griffiths. But
when Armstrong found himself alone in his business, it
undoubtedly began to fall off. It was a pity, from Armstrong's point of view, that Mr. Martin was there to conduct
actively the business brought to the old-established firm;
if he had not been there circumstances might almost have
forced them to make some arrangement with Armstrong.
Anyhow, when the war was over, and people were beginning to take up the threads again, there were these two
solicitors in Hay, their offices facing each other across the
street, and there for the moment we will leave them.

III

Armstrong was a popular man in Hay. On his return
from the war he called himself Major Armstrong, and
attached much importance to his military rank. He was
very active in all the affairs of the place, and secured,
among other appointments, that of clerk to the justices,
which introduced his finger into many small local pies. Mr.
Martin was not so popular. It was not in his character to
seek popularity, and he suffered, as a result of his services
to his country, from a form of paralysis which affected one
side of his face, and sometimes gave people the impression
that he was smiling when he was not. He was a quiet man,
and lived his own life quietly. Armstrong, although he took
pains to ingratiate himself with everyone, was not at home

the martial figure that his military career and gallant adventures might have led one to expect. It was common knowledge that he was, in fact, henpecked. The late Mrs. Armstrong was a person of peculiar character. She was both cultivated and clever, played the piano extremely well, and had earned the reputation with everyone who had any knowledge of her of being a really good woman. She was, however, notoriously cranky, and extremely severe. She brought up her children with devotion, indeed, but with a strict and sombre austerity, and her husband was ruled with a rod of iron. Until the war broke his boundaries and enlarged his horizon little Armstrong (for he was a very little man, weighing only some 7 stone) had no kind of liberty at home, and, except for certain furtive, amorous adventures of which I have heard, he was obliged to live under the strict conditions imposed by his wife. These conditions were of an unusual severity. No wine or alcohol was admitted to the house. If at the table of some neighbour he was offered wine, his wife would interpose with a negative on his account, except now and then when she had been known to say, "I think you may have a glass of port, Herbert; it will do your cold good." If he was smoking as he came along the road, and his wife came in sight, the cigar or pipe had to be hastily put away, and he was only allowed to smoke in one room of his house called "Mayfield." On one occasion, at a tennis party, she called to him in the middle of a set that it was time to go home. "Six o'clock, Herbert; how can you expect punctuality in the servants if the master is late for his meals?" On another similar occasion, in publicly summoning him to come home, she reminded him that it was his "bath night." Such a state of affairs seems fantastic, but there is no doubt that it existed. For whatever reason, she had him thoroughly under her thumb, and (no doubt for his own good) was determined to keep him there. People liked the little man, and were sorry for him; but, however hard upon him they may have thought Mrs. Armstrong was, it did not diminish

—who knows that it did not enhance?—that undoubted respect in which she was held by her neighbours.

IV

This, then, was the course of the life of these people in Hay to the outward eye. Local events came and went. Local gossips talked of this or that person's affairs; people attended little parties, came and went as they do in all such places. Illness is always a topic for gossip in small country towns, and among the figures that moved through the busy life of the place none was more universally regarded with interest and affection than Dr. "Tom" Hincks, who had succeeded to his father's practice in the place and was known and trusted and liked for miles around. The big, upright figure with the open countenance and the charming smile was a familiar sight. Whatever he was doing, hunting up on the hills or shooting in the countryside, Dr. "Tom" always put his patients first; and often, if he were going out for a day's shooting, would get up at five in the morning and attend to his medical work and be busy on it up till midnight after he had come home. His presence in a house would indicate to the gossips that somebody was ill. It was rumoured in August, 1920, that Mrs. Armstrong was in indifferent health, and that her eccentricities had increased; and, sure enough, on August 22, 1920, Dr. Hincks himself was seen taking her away in a motor-car to Gloucester, where she was placed in Barnwood Private Asylum. Here was food for conversation. It was known that she suffered from acute depression and some kind of nervous affection of the hands which prevented her from playing the piano, and people's sympathy with her husband already increased when this new trial became known.

During her absence the little man enjoyed, it is true, a certain freedom. People were kind to him and asked him out. Heads, if they were wagged, were wagged in secret. Then, six months later, it was known that Mrs. Armstrong was much better, and was coming home. And in January, 1921, she came home, but began to fail again. A mental nurse was installed, and in February, 1921, people heard that Mrs. Armstrong was very ill, and that Dr. Hincks was calling every day. And on February 22 this poor lady died, and, a few days later, was buried at Cusop Church-yard, near by her home. A friend, who was one of the four who attended the funeral, told me that Armstrong seemed quite unaffected, and was chatting about fishing rights while the coffin was being carried down. And on the following Sunday at the little village church, where the service was made a kind of memorial to the good lady, he read the lessons (so the sexton told me) with great eloquence and feeling.

v

And so life was resumed once more; Major Armstrong took a new lease of it, and gave little dinner-parties, at which alcohol was no longer banned. People came and went, got ill and got well, and so on. After one of Armstrong's little dinner-parties the local inspector of taxes, who had done justice to the excellent madeira provided by his host, was taken very ill on the way home and had a very bad night; and people who knew of it rather smiled. There was a good deal of illness in the autumn of 1921. Mr. Martin, for example, was ill for several days, and had to have Dr. Hincks in constant attendance. Now among those people who did not accept Major Armstrong's invitations were Mr. and Mrs. Martin. But it was characteristic of the little man that he was not easily rebuffed, and so he gave continued invitations, and appeared to want to be friendly and sociable, but could only on one occasion induce Martin to come to his house, and they had tea together. When further invitations to tea failed, Armstrong tried inviting the Martins to dinner, but even that was refused, and it was thought that business relations must be getting rather strained.

And then, suddenly, a series of bombshells fell. On New Year's Day, 1922, the town was dumbfounded to hear that Major Armstrong had been arrested the day before and charged with attempting to murder Mr. Martin. This roused the greatest indignation. People went so far as to suggest that it had been engineered by Martin on account of business rivalry. But still more astounding events happened the next day. Strange doctors came to town; it was known that something was happening up at Cusop Churchyard; and then that Mrs. Armstrong's body had been exhumed that very morning and was being examined in a little cottage near the churchyard. Reporters descended apparently from the skies. Sensation after sensation was reported. Gossip upon gossip multiplied, and through five long months, until Armstrong was executed, the town was a centre of sensation and excitement such as is rarely experienced in such a place.

VI

That was the outward course of events. Now let us glance at the events a little beneath the surface as they appeared to those two or three intimately engaged with the persons chiefly concerned, so that later we may go deeper still and examine some matters which were known to nobody at the time except possibly Armstrong himself.

When Armstrong was suddenly arrested on December 31, 1921, there were five people only in Hay who were not surprised. They were Dr. Hincks, Mr. and Mrs. Martin, Mr. Davies (Mr. Martin's father-in-law), and Mr. Trevor Griffiths. For the greater part of two months these people had been certain that Armstrong was trying to poison Mr. Martin, and that he had poisoned his own wife. They had been in communication with the Home Office, who had enjoined upon them the strictest secrecy and the necessity for not letting Armstrong have a glimmering of an idea that he was suspected. It was a dramatic and eerie situation for these people, and the last three weeks must have been extremely trying.

Consider the facts. Only two months before Martin, after repeated invitations, had gone to tea with Armstrong at his house. There was a business difficulty between them, and he thought that Armstrong wished to discuss it, although, as a matter of fact, he never alluded to it. During tea he had handed Martin a buttered scone with the apology, "Excuse my fingers," and Martin had eaten that, as well as some currant loaf. He had hardly got home before he was seized with the most violent pains, with vomiting and diarrhœa, which continued throughout the night and reduced him swiftly to a condition of extreme weakness. Dr. Hincks was called in, and saw the usual symptoms of a severe bilious attack, and prescribed accordingly. But, as the sickness continued, he was (fortunately) not entirely satisfied, and he had an analysis made, and found in the sample submitted that there was one-thirty-third of a grain of arsenic. This set him thinking and pondering, and one day, riding on horseback over the hills to visit a distant patient, and revolving in his mind the circumstances attending the death of Mrs. Armstrong, the key to the whole situation flashed on him. That neuritis of hers, which they had all regarded as a merely functional disorder, had not been functional but organic; it was peripheral neuritis—one of the symptoms of arsenical poisoning. He remembered all the other symptoms. Vomiting, the peculiarity known as "high steppage" gait, discoloration of the skin, etc., etc.—all symptoms of arsenical poisoning. What Martin was suffering from, Mrs. Armstrong had died of. And if in a small liquid sample taken from Mr. Martin one-thirty-third of a grain of arsenic had been found, what might be found in the body of Mrs. Armstrong? The more he thought of it the plainer it became. He wrote at once to the doctors at Barnwood Asylum, and they, too, realized that they had been deceived as to the cause of Mrs. Armstrong's physical illness. They remembered how the symptoms had diminished during her stay in the asylum and reappeared after her return home; they, too, realized that they had mistaken organic for functional disease, and (in the complete absence of suspicion) missed the diagnosis which would have put them on the right track. The facts were placed before the Home Office, and the slow but certain wheels of the criminal law began to revolve. Stiffly and hesitatingly they moved at first, as the Director of Public Prosecutions began to make his own independent inquiries; but ever increased in pace and smoothness and momentum, until in the dock of His Majesty's Assizes for the county of Herefordshire they flung off Armstrong into the outer darkness of shameful extinction.

The Home Office was, naturally, slow to move at the beginning; it does not do to suspect everyone against whom some private malice or feud may inspire or suggest suspicion. Moreover, in a recent case of poisoning alleged against a solicitor in Wales the defendant had been acquitted. It was probable that the authorities were determined not to set the law in motion on such a charge unless they were absolutely certain that suspicion was properly founded, and that the case would be proved; for if it is a terrible thing that a murderer should escape, it is an equally terrible thing that an innocent man should be put on trial for his life. Therefore, the first steps were taken cautiously; but to Dr. Hincks and the Martins, who were convinced of Armstrong's guilt, and certain that he was engaged in a persistent attempt to poison Martin, the machinery seemed to move slowly indeed. One must consider Martin's position. He was afraid of Armstrong. He remembered that sinister occasion when he had yielded to Armstrong's entreaties to go to tea with him, and the agonies that had followed; and here was the same man daily ringing him up and insisting that he should go to tea with him again. The two were solicitors for the vendor and purchaser of some property respectively. Armstrong had failed to complete; Martin was pressing for the return of the deposit—some

five hundred pounds—but neither completion nor deposit
was forthcoming from Armstrong—only invitations to tea.
If it were not such a grim story there would be something
comic in this almost furious bombardment of tea invitations
across the village street in Hay.

"Will you come to tea this afternoon?" telephones
Armstrong. "Can't come to tea," replies Martin, "but I
will look in afterwards about six." "Oh, never mind," says
Armstrong. "Any day will do. Come to tea to-morrow
instead." Martin, quaking with apprehension, does not go
to tea to-morrow. The telephone bell rings again. "Why
did you not come to tea?" says Armstrong. "Tea has been
waiting for you for half an hour."

Tea and telephones, these were the weapons with which
this sinister warfare was waged. Then, as Martin would
not go to tea at Mayfield on his way home through Cusop
Dingle, as Mahomet would not come to the mountain, the
tea mountain was brought to Mahomet. Tea was started
at Armstrong's office; butter was brought from Mayfield,
scones sent over from the little café across the road. The
telephone now asked Mr. Martin to come across and have
tea at the office. In vain was the net spread in the sight of
poor Mr. Martin; but he was hard put to it to find excuses
for not crossing the road and taking his tea with Armstrong.
So in sheer self-defence, though, I imagine, with poor appe-
tite, he started having tea in his own office, in order to have
an excuse for not going across the road. And so one pictures, amid this furious gale of invitations, these two men
sitting on either side of the street having their tea, or unable
to have it; Armstrong furiously drinking his, when Martin
would not come; Martin distastefully not taking his, in
order to say that he had had it. Martin confided to Dr.
Hincks that he could not stand it much longer. "Whatever
you do," they said, "keep away from Armstrong's house.
And under no circumstances eat or drink anything in his
presence." The police were making secret visits, chiefly at
night, to Hay and insisting on the same policy; above all,

Armstrong was not to be alarmed. "All very well," says poor Martin, "but he is bombarding me with invitations to tea; every time I see him he darts across the road, 'Why not come to tea?' And I have run out of excuses." "Hold on a bit longer," they tell him. And he and Mrs. Martin actually took it in turns to keep awake at night, haunted by one knows not what grim, beckoning spectre with a tea-cup in its hand. And so Armstrong was at last put to the necessity of asking Mr. and Mrs. Martin to dinner. It was expensive, of course, but it need only happen once. Martin made some kind of a temporizing answer, but on the day that the invitation fell due Armstrong was already in the hands of the police, and Mr. and Mrs. Martin could breathe freely.

The ordeal of Dr. Hincks was to last a day longer. He was in a very peculiar position, owing partly to the courage and integrity of his own character. Armstrong was his patient, and he had been attending him and giving treatment for venereal disease periodically for some time; and while he was attending him he was already in communication with the police on the subject of his arrest. In his own opinion (and I think most people would agree) he had no alternative in either case. He believed Armstrong to be a murderer and wished him to be arrested; but every man is presumed innocent until he is proved guilty, and there was no valid reason why he should discontinue his treatment and so drive his patient to the necessity of confiding in another doctor. But, although Armstrong had been arrested on the charge of attempting to murder Martin, the real case against him was that he had murdered Mrs. Armstrong, and until her body had been exhumed Dr. Hincks must have been in considerable suspense. Had that body been found free from arsenic he would have been in the position of having made unwarranted accusations against his friend and patient; and he might have walked out of Hay, which had been the scene of his work for thirty years, and his home for fifty. But when, on the day following the

arrest of Armstrong, Mrs. Armstrong's coffin was opened
the first glance told Dr. Hincks and Dr. Spilsbury that his
suspicions were correct. The state of preservation of the
remains told them that at once, and the fact was confirmed
a little later when the analysis of Mr. Webster revealed the
actual presence of a greater quantity of arsenic then he had
ever found in a poisoned body.

It cannot be doubted that Dr. Hincks acted with a courage worthy of the highest traditions of his profession. He
had been mistaken about Mrs. Armstrong's illness and the
cause of her death, as had the other doctors who had
attended her; but as soon as his suspicions were aroused
he shouldered the burden of the inevitable consequences,
and did his duty to society.

VII

The reader must now be informed of another cause of
suspicion against Armstrong. About a month before the
episode of the tea-time attempt, and soon after Martin's
arrival in Hay and marriage to Miss Davies, he had one
morning received a parcel containing a box of chocolates.
Neither he nor his wife was in the habit of eating chocolates,
and the box was put away until some days later, when they
were having friends to dinner, and Mrs. Martin put some
into a bon-bon dish. There was no clue as to where the
chocolates came from, and after the party those that were
left were put back into the box. Someone was taken ill after
that dinner-party, and later the chocolates were examined,
and it was found that some of them had a small hole drilled
in the base and that arsenic had been inserted. The dia-
meter of the hole exactly fitted the nozzle of the instrument
that Armstrong afterwards alleged that he used to inject
arsenic into the roots of dandelions. Another case which
subsequently brought Armstrong under suspicion was that
of Mr. Davies, an estate agent at Hereford, who had some
controversial business with Armstrong; who came to Hay,

had lunch or tea with Armstrong, and was taken ill with acute abdominal pain on his return home. He was operated on for appendicitis, and died, the cause of death being (I believe) certified as peritonitis following acute appendicitis. It is possible that in certain circumstances the cause of his death might have been the subject of further investigation.

VIII

When Armstrong appeared before the magistrate at his own bench in Hay, his place as clerk was taken by his elderly colleague, the clerk to the bench at Talgarth, to whose office he had himself aspired already. This gentleman had been one of the dinner-party of four after which the inspector of taxes was taken so ill, and it is possible that the inspector had suffered in his stead. It is said that there was a somewhat rich vein of comedy in the way he handled Armstrong at these proceedings. The prisoner himself, not to be outdone, offered to assist his elderly colleague, whose infirmity hampered him in the execution of his onerous duties. Anyhow, the usual depositions were taken, and Armstrong was committed for trial at the next Herefordshire Assizes, the defence being reserved. The trial began on April 3, 1922, before Mr. Justice Darling, who was then on his last circuit prior to retirement. The Attorney-General, Sir Ernest Pollock, K.C. (afterwards Lord Hanworth), assisted by Mr. C. H. Vachell, K.C., and Mr. St. John Micklethwait, represented the Crown, and the defence was conducted by Sir Henry Curtis Bennett, K.C., Mr. S. R. C. Bosanquet, and Mr. E. A. Godson. The Grand Jury, on Mr. Justice Darling's advice, had thrown out the bill as to the attempted poisoning by means of a box of chocolates, there being insufficient evidence to connect the prisoner with the sending of the box.

The proceedings began with a long and important argument as to whether the evidence as regards what we may call the Martin case was admissible. Many cases were cited,

and Mr. Justice Darling finally decided that the evidence
was admissible on the ground that it showed that the use
of arsenic for poisoning human beings as well as dandelions
had occurred to the prisoner's mind. This decision was of
the greatest importance. If it had been wrong, and the
Court of Appeal had held that the evidence was, in fact,
inadmissible, the conviction of Armstrong would have been
quashed, and he would have been released. On the other
hand, without this evidence it seemed unlikely that there
would be a verdict for conviction, and Mr. Justice Darling
was already of opinion that the case was of a kind in which
it was desirable, in order to get at the truth, to have as
much evidence as possible as to the surrounding circumstances. As it turned out, his decision was right, and was
upheld by the Court of Appeal. The greater part of the
evidence at the trial was of a medical nature, and was of
the unsavoury kind usually associated with cases of arsenical poisoning. The suggestion of the defence was that Mrs.
Armstrong herself had deliberately taken arsenic, that she
was of unsound mind and suicidal tendencies, that her husband had no motive for murdering her, and that there was
no evidence that he had ever administered arsenic. There
was a further medical defence presented by Dr. F. S. Toogood that Mrs. Armstrong suffered from auto-intoxication
when she went into the mental hospital, and that arsenic
had nothing to do with her condition, and that there was
nothing in the conditions inconsistent with her having had
no arsenic whatever up to February 16, when one poisonous dose was taken which caused her death. To account
for the discrepancy of these conditions with the time taken
for the arsenic to reach the parts of the body as found at
the post-mortem examination, he put forward the ingenious
theory that a large part of the arsenic had become encysted,
or retained in a kind of capsule attached to the wall of the
stomach. He cited in support of his theory the case of the
Duc de Praslin, who was alleged to have been poisoned
in 1846, but Mr. Justice Darling knew all about the Duc de

Praslin, and also that the evidence of his case was known to have been falsified and misrepresented, so he was able to dispose of this ingenious theory in his summing up. The only comment to be made on Dr. Toogood's evidence was that it was not good enough.

IX

Perhaps the most dramatic thing in the course of a trial that took place throughout in an atmosphere of tense emotion was the disclosure by Sir Henry Curtis Bennett that after Armstrong's arrest a packet of arsenic had been found in a drawer in his bureau which the police had already searched without result. It seems that after Armstrong's arrest he told his solicitor about this packet, which represented the residue of the white arsenic that he had bought at Davies's shop. His solicitor went on his instructions to Mayfield, looked in the bureau and, like the police, failed to find the packet. Then he went again with his clerk, and he described in his evidence how they found the packet of arsenic " caught up " at the back of a drawer. They applied for a list of the articles found by the police, in order to ascertain whether this packet had been seen by them or not; it had not, and so they did not disclose its presence until Sir Henry Curtis Bennett produced it so dramatically at the trial itself. At first sight there seems something peculiar about the discovery of this packet, and the reader will naturally ask, was it put there by the defence, and, if so, for what purpose? Or was it put there by the agents of the police, and left as a trap, and, if so, for what purpose? It seems a little mysterious; and the importance of it does not seem sufficient to account for the sensation caused by it. But I believe the facts of the matter to be simply those revealed in the evidence; Armstrong did remember it, and told his solicitor about it, and it was first overlooked and ultimately found, and the finding not communicated to the police. It is interesting to see the different use made of such

a piece of evidence and the comments of Lord Darling, Sir
Ernest Pollock, and Sir Henry Curtis Bennett respectively.
Lord Darling treated it as a very damaging piece of evidence, and commented on Armstrong's alleged failure to
remember it; Sir Henry Curtis Bennett went so far as to
say that it might save Armstrong's life, as accounting for
the remainder of the purchase of arsenic, half of which he
alleged he used in making up the little packets for poisoning dandelions. Its chief interest now lies in the example it gives of the ingenuity of a clever counsel in
interpreting every fact as favourably as possible to his
client.

Armstrong gave evidence on his own behalf with the
same calmness that he maintained throughout the trial, and
was quite unshaken until, after a severe cross-examination
by the Attorney-General and a re-examination by his own
counsel, he was taken in hand by the judge, who, in a few
masterly and persistent questions, revealed Armstrong's
inability either to explain the little packet of arsenic found
on him at his arrest, or to conceal the fact that there was
another packet hidden in the desk in his bureau which the
police did not find when they searched. The judge's questions also made it difficult for anyone to believe that
Armstrong really did, for the purpose of poisoning twenty
individual dandelions, make up twenty individual packets
of white arsenic. These questions shook the prisoner, and,
I imagine, really shattered the case for the defence. Anyone
who reads them, and Armstrong's method of dealing with
them, can have little doubt that they went to the root of
the matter of his guilt far more certainly than the arsenic
ever went to the roots of his dandelions. Sir Henry Curtis
Bennett made a very effective and eloquent speech for the
defence, and the Attorney-General's reply was a masterly
example of its kind. Armstrong sat apparently unmoved
through everything, with blue eyes staring in front of him
throughout the summing up.

Severe as the judge's summing up was, the general

opinion was that Armstrong would be acquitted, and the betting was in favour of acquittal. Sir Henry Curtis Bennett himself was so confident that he went for a walk, expecting to come back either to hear the verdict for acquittal or to meet Armstrong himself and find that he had already been released. As it was, when he got back to Hereford, the newsboys were crying in the streets the paper announcing the verdict "Guilty." A regrettable indiscretion on the part of a juryman and a London evening newspaper revealed to the public the fact that when the jury retired to consider their verdict the foreman asked everyone to write his verdict on a slip of paper, and that eleven bore the word "Guilty" and one "Not proven"; and when the foreman announced the result the man who had written "Not proven" said, "Well, Tom, you know what 'Not proven' means. I really believe the man is guilty." After which the foreman, finding they were all agreed, was alleged to have said, "We have heard enough of the case, and we needn't discuss it any more. Let's have a quiet smoke before we go back into Court." This unexpected glimpse into the methods of a jury consisting of ten farmers and two professional men is undoubtedly interesting, and seems to indicate a degree of common sense which should go far to refute the theories of those who think that an ordinary jury is not a satisfactory tribunal for the testing of circumstantial evidence. But the publication of this story was severely censured at the time by several eminent judges.

In due time the case came before the Court of Criminal Appeal, presided over by the Lord Chief Justice, who sat with Mr. Justice Avory and Mr. Justice Shearman. The appeal was dismissed, and a fortnight later, on May 31, 1922, Armstrong was duly hanged at Gloucester, having made no confession. His attitude to the religious administrations of his clerical friends was described as being one of "respectful attention." He was visited by Mr. Matthews, his solicitor, and Mr. Chevalier, a Liverpool solicitor who had been trusted and esteemed by Mrs. Armstrong, and (no doubt for her sake and the children's) did what he could to arrange Armstrong's somewhat tangled affairs. Death was dealt to him on that May morning, while the birds in Cusop Dingle were singing about the house where his children were awaking, with the swift and merciful efficiency of modern methods; and for the sins that he committed he paid up to the full measure of his capacity to pay.

X

Armstrong's presence was characterized by neatness and smartness of appearance and alacrity of demeanour. He was very small, but so well proportioned that he did not seem small, unless he was standing beside a person of normal height. He was voluble and egotistical, regarding himself and his affairs as of great importance; his manners were excellent. Some people found him simply a bore; others, among whom were a certain number of women, found him attractive. The most remarkable thing about him was his eyes. They were light blue, the colour of forget-me-nots, and they had a glittering brilliancy, almost as though there was a light behind them. This, it will be remembered, was also a characteristic of George Joseph Smith, the man who had a habit of marrying women with a little money and drowning them in a bath; and, I doubt not, of many other scoundrels.

XI

In cases where so much of the evidence is circumstantial it is generally considered necessary to have ample proof not only of the cause of death, or of the actual giving of poison, but also that the defendant had it in his possession, knew how to use it, and had both motive and opportunity for using it. Armstrong was an old hand with arsenic. He was interested in his garden, waged a continuous warfare against dandelions and plantains, and always had stocks of weed-killer, which is a preparation of arsenic, in hand. In addition to this he bought arsenic himself and made up his own weed-killer; still further, and this was a significant fact, he bought a quantity of white arsenic in the January preceding Mrs. Armstrong's removal to the asylum, and bought it from the local chemist, Davies—Mr. Martin's father-in-law. It is this white arsenic which he is alleged to have used to poison Mrs. Armstrong and Mr. Martin. As to opportunity, there was no doubt, and it was not contested, that he often sat with his wife when she was ill and, in the absence of the nurse, gave her whatever nourishment she was having. As to motive, however, there was a difference of opinion. Sir Henry Curtis Bennett was very impressive on this subject of absence of motive; and, indeed, to any ordinary mind there would seem to be no motive great enough to account for so monstrous a crime. But motives which would not be sufficient for ordinary people were, apparently, sufficient for Armstrong. With regard to his wife there was a financial motive—miserable enough, it is true, for the lady possessed only about two thousand pounds in the world; but the incident of the will indicated that Armstrong attached importance to it. While he was away at the war she made a brief will leaving everything she had to her children, with a small legacy to a Miss Pearce, and nothing to her husband. But soon after he came back she signed, or was alleged to have signed, a new will in which nothing was left to her children or Miss Pearce, and everything to her husband. This will was in the prisoner's own handwriting, and, if the signature was not a forgery, it was almost certainly obtained under a mistaken notion as to what the document was, for the will was improperly witnessed, the witnesses signing neither in the presence of the testator nor of each other. Armstrong's story of this will was given in his evidence; its existence, I am afraid we must admit, shows that he had a financial interest in the death of his wife. To that must be added the fact that he was in financial difficulties at the time, and that he died insolvent.

We have seen what kind of a woman Mrs. Armstrong was, and that Armstrong's life with her was not what one might call joyful. There is further to be considered the fact that he had contracted an intimacy—of what degree is really of no great importance—with a lady unnamed, who gave evidence at the trial; she came and spent a night at Hay soon after his wife's death—presumably to see his house and the children; and within a month or two of the death he had asked her to marry him, although at the time of the arrest she had, apparently, not decided to do so. These, then, were the motives which induced him to embark on the campaign of cumulative poisoning in minute doses which had been going on for some time before Mrs. Armstrong's removal to the asylum. There is a difficulty as to the administration of the large dose which was evidently given within a few hours of her being removed to Barnwood. One may well ask what can have been his object in administering a large and fatal dose to a woman who had just been examined by two doctors and certified as mentally insane, but physically in ordinary health. Supposing, as might well have happened, that Mrs. Armstrong, who was taken violently ill just before starting for the asylum, and had presumably got rid of the greater portion of the dose, had died in the motor-car on the way to Gloucester, there would have had to be an inquest; neither Dr. Hincks nor the other doctor who certified her would have given a death certificate in such circumstances; and a post-mortem examination would have revealed the presence of arsenic. One may well wonder why Armstrong took such risks. It can only be assumed that, in the case of the dose being successful, his defence would have been that the poor lady, on hearing that she was going to be taken to the asylum, decided to commit suicide. A possible motive (not put forward by the prosecution) for Armstrong's desire that his wife should be discharged from the asylum, and not merely sent home on leave, was that in the latter case she would still have been under a certificate of lunacy, and therefore not qualified to make the new will which he drafted and which she signed.

The delusions from which she suffered were of a sad and pathetic nature. She, whose life was governed by a sense of duty, went about weighed down by the fantastic belief that she did not do her duty by her husband and children, and that she had committed some criminal act for which she could be arrested. She was also under what was certified as the " untrue dèlusion " that she was being poisoned; but in the light of later knowledge this appears to have been no delusion but simple fact.

A terrible possibility here presents itself. It was suggested to me, by one who saw her constantly during this period, that she knew she was being poisoned, and that in her strange mental condition she felt that she must not, for the sake of her children, reveal what she knew and incriminate her husband. If there is any possibility of truth in that view (and only those who knew her and were with her can judge), it raises her martyrdom to a point of heroic tragedy such as has surely never been recorded before. I can only say for myself, having pondered the matter considerably, that I have no kind of certainty about it either way, and that I only hope it is not true. Another of her " delusions " was that Dr. Hincks did not know what was the matter with her; and this, as he would be the first to admit, is not entirely baseless. That at this time she took a dislike to and mistrust in doctors generally on the grounds that they " did not know what was the matter with her " might add some plausibility to the ghastly possibility that I have suggested. I am bound to suggest it, because the person who holds that view has a more intimate knowledge of the circumstances than anyone else living.

As to the second large dose of arsenic, from which Mrs. Armstrong died, and which, according to the defence, was administered by herself, there is no evidence that in her enfeebled condition she could have moved from her bed to get such a dose, even if she knew where to get it, for a period much in excess of the twenty-four hours preceding her death. Although Sir Henry Curtis Bennett did his best to produce medical evidence that the fatal dose must have been taken earlier than twenty-four hours before death, it did not convince the jury; and, in the light of the evidence of Sir Henry Willcox and Dr. Spilsbury, it will hardly convince the reader. Presumably, like all arsenic poisoners, Armstrong got tired of the small doses and decided to hasten matters, and to put an end to the situation once and for all.

Mr. Justice Darling dealt thoroughly with the prisoner's story of having actually wrapped twenty little packets for the purpose of poisoning twenty dandelions. It seems unlikely, and the jury disbelieved it. These were the kind of little packets that were handy for using at the tea-table; and, as we know, one of them was actually found in his pocket at the time of his arrest, ready, no doubt, for Mr. Martin should his reluctance to come to tea be overcome. There is only this to be said, that people who knew Armstrong well say that it was just the kind of thing he would have done. He was a fiddling and pernickety little man, who liked messing about with chemicals and apparatus; and I have had shown to me the little instrument which he said he used for injecting arsenic powder into dandelion roots—a kind of small syringe with a fine nozzle. Indeed, he gave it to Dr. Hincks with some other hospital apparatus, after Mrs. Armstrong's death, as something he had no more use for. But it is significant that the little nozzle exactly fitted the little hole that was drilled in the chocolates sent to Mrs. Martin.

XII

I have sat through a summer morning on a chair on the tennis lawn of the house which used to be called Mayfield. The dandelions were thicker than ever, and the plantains had, at the time of my visit, taken almost complete possession of half of the lawn. The sun shone, the doors and windows were wide open, so that the summer breeze stirred through the house, and the voices of children at play sounded in the precincts. A saner and more normal life, and a happier set of children, had taken possession of the place. But my thoughts were with those other little children whose voices, more repressed and not quite so happy, had sounded there at the time of this story. It is the presence of those children that to me at any rate invests this crime with a peculiar dreadfulness. And in considering the endless puzzle of what it is in one man that, side by side with ordinary human qualities, makes him capable of fiendish cruelty and puts him into the class which we call criminal, I am impelled to the conclusion that what makes a poisoner differ from the normal man is not so much a positive as a negative quality. It is the absence of something from his moral make-up, rather than the presence of something, that seems to me to make the difference. And in this case I would say that what Armstrong and people like him lack is imagination. They see things and actions objectively, not subjectively. Otherwise, how would it be possible for a man engaged with life in all its ordinary relationships not to recoil from contemplation of the effect of his conduct on those little lives? There is something innocent in the worst of us; and no one can live in the company of little children without being aware, were it only wistfully, of the morning freshness and beauty of their outlook. It is easier to understand a man murdering his children in insane desperation than cold-bloodedly scheming and contriving actions which could only blot out the sunshine of their lives in darkness and shame. I am driven to believe, therefore, that this man was deprived of the power of realizing or imagining what might happen, or what must happen, to his children as a consequence of his actions.

FIELD AND GRAY
(1920)

By Winifred Duke

I

ON Saturday, August 14, 1920, a middle-aged Scotswoman named Flora Munro, the widow of a Brighton coal merchant, left London for a holiday in her native country. She acted as housekeeper to a family called Sinclair, living in South Kensington, and had been several years in their employment. Her only child, a daughter of seventeen, Irene Violet, made her home with her mother, and went daily to her work as a shorthand-typist.

Mrs. Munro travelled by sea, being seen off at Wapping Pier by her sister, Mrs. Winter, and Irene. Aunt and niece parted company after the boat had sailed about midday. Irene returned to South Kensington, where she spent the week-end in completing preparations for her own holiday which was due to begin on Monday, 16th August. There had been some discussion concerning the desirability of the girl accompanying her mother, but Irene preferred to go to the seaside by herself. The previous summer she had stayed at Brighton alone, and this year she decided on Eastbourne for her fortnight's liberty. She knew nobody there, and, so far as was known, had no motive in selecting it above any other holiday resort. She did not make any inquiries or arrangements beforehand about accommodation, though Mrs. Sinclair, her mother's employer, gave her the address of rooms, telling her that if the landlady could not take her in she would recommend her somewhere else.

Irene Munro rose at 5.30 a.m. on Monday, went to Victoria Station, and there caught the 7.20 train, reaching

Eastbourne about ten o'clock. From a letter written by her to her mother three days later, it appeared that on her arrival she found holiday accommodation at a premium, and spent the greater part of the Monday in a vain quest for lodgings. About 4.30 in the afternoon she was walking along Seaside, a road in a working-class district, when a card advertising a bed-sitting-room, displayed in the window of a small end house, attracted her attention. She rang the bell at 393 Seaside, and inquired of the landlady, Mrs. Wynniatt, whether she could put her up. Irene Munro explained that she was a typist on holiday and not in a position to pay a great deal. Mrs. Wynniatt showed her the room, a single-bedded one on the ground floor, and agreed to let it to her for a week from the following day (Tuesday, August 17). The charge for the room, bed and breakfast, was 30s. When paying Mrs. Wynniatt a pound as deposit, Irene Munro took the money out of a brown leather purse which she kept in a handbag. The landlady did not bestow any particular attention on this bag, nor was she able to describe it afterwards, but she received the impression, subsequently found to be erroneous, that the purse contained a number of Treasury notes, at least seven or eight. The room was occupied for the Monday night, so Mrs. Wynniatt escorted Irene Munro to a neighbour's house a few doors away, and Mrs. Baulcombe promised to take her in until next morning. After these arrangements were concluded, Irene went back to Eastbourne, and did not reappear at 1 Norman Cottages, Wartling Road, until between 9.30 and 10 at night. She retired at once to bed, having presumably had supper in the town.

Next day (17th) the visitor paid half a crown for her night's accommodation and left Mrs. Baulcombe's at 9.15 a.m. The only person she spoke of to her temporary hostess was her mother, a brief mention that she had written to inform her of her safe arrival. At 9.30 a young naval stoker, named William Putland, enjoying sixteen days' leave at Eastbourne, chanced to be on the beach, a few

hundred yards from the respective houses of Mrs. Baulcombe and Mrs. Wynniatt. He was one of a crowd of
people watching a seaplane taking up passengers. As it
returned to the shed, Putland noticed a girl lying on the
beach close beside the latter building. She was wearing a
green, three-quarter-length velour coat, with a collar, cuffs,
and border of black fur. Putland was near enough to see
her face when she stood up, but did not particularly note
her features. The vivid colour of the coat, however, attracted
his attention, and when he saw it on two subsequent
occasions he had no doubt that each time the wearer was
this same girl.

Irene Munro, dressed in a short-sleeved frock trimmed
with gold braid, arrived at Mrs. Wynniatt's about 10.30 and
breakfasted there. In the course of the morning she went
to fetch her suitcase from Mrs. Baulcombe's, and returned
with it at 12.30. She stayed in till 2.30, when she announced
her intention of having some lunch, presumably in Eastbourne. She did not come back to her lodgings until ten
o'clock at night.

The girl's movements, later carefully checked, revealed
that on the Tuesday she paid a couple of visits to a jewel-
ler's shop in Eastbourne where she bought a gold pencil-
case, alleging that it was a present for her uncle. She
reported the transaction to Mrs. Wynniatt, but the latter
was not shown the article as it had been sent direct from
the shop to the recipient. In Irene Munro's letter to her
mother, written, as previously mentioned, on Thursday
(19th), she stated that on the Tuesday she had been to
Beachy Head, and she also told Mrs. Wynniatt this after
her return. To neither did she say whether she went in the
company of anybody, but the landlady took it for granted
that she was by herself. She explained that she had lost her
way and taken a shortcut across the golf-links. On Wednesday (18th) she went out after breakfast, reappearing
about 1 p.m. During the afternoon she left her lodgings
between two and three o'clock and did not return until

10 p.m. She informed Mrs. Wynniatt that she had been to Pevensey, and seemed amused at having lost a heel and a button off one shoe. Directly after she came in she went out again to the post, but was only absent for a few minutes.

On Thursday (19th) Mrs. Wynniatt was told by Irene Munro about 10.30 a.m. that she thought of walking to Hampden Park. This was inland, roughly a mile or two away, and lay in a quite opposite direction to that which she was subsequently proved to have taken later in the day. During the morning she wrote to her mother, and mentioned in the letter that she was sitting on the beach as she penned it. Between 1.30 and 1.45 she came back to 393 Seaside, and remained there until she went out once more about 2.45. Since the beginning of the week the house had been in the hands of painters. These two men had seen Irene Munro and knew that she was Mrs. Wynniatt's lodger. One of them, Frederick George Rogers, happened to be working at the gate and opened it for the girl's exit. She walked away in the direction of the Archery, a tavern some 69 yards distant from the house. A few minutes later she reappeared and explained to Rogers that she had come to fetch her coat. Rogers asked whether she would require one as it was a warm afternoon, but Irene replied that she might be out late, whereupon he answered, "I think you are wise." This remark was audible to Mrs. Wynniatt, who was in a room adjoining Irene's. She heard the girl go into her bedroom, and after remaining there for a brief time, leave the house again. Irene was noticed by Rogers to be now wearing a green coat, and he also saw that she took the same direction as she had done just before, i.e., towards the Archery.

Rogers's fellow-workman, a youth named Verrall, was on a ladder, painting the outside wall of the house. A garden and a short passage divided it from the road. From his elevation he saw Irene Munro go out, return, depart again, and a little later the sound of a laugh attracted his attention to three people walking past. Verrall looked down over the intervening shrubs and recognized Irene Munro as the person who had laughed. She was with two men. Both were unknown to Verrall, but he saw the girl quite plainly when she turned her face towards the house in going by. Verrall was unable afterwards to describe her dress, nor did he see the face of either of her companions. He received the impression that both wore grey suits and no hats. All three went off in the direction of the Crumbles, an unfrequented part of the shore between Eastbourne and Pevensey Bay.

Irene Munro had said nothing to her landlady about not coming back to her lodgings. Her luggage and small personal possessions were left there. Mrs. Wynniatt expected her at any time, but the afternoon and evening wore on and she did not return. The landlady stayed up till midnight, by which hour there was still no sign of her, and she continued absent the whole of the following day (Friday). Mrs. Wynniatt was a busy woman. She did all the cooking for the household, and herself waited on her lodgers, so she had had very little conversation with the young girl, who did not even give her London address. Beyond alluding to the nature of her work, and the fact that her mother was in Scotland and had wanted her to go with her, Irene Munro had told Mrs. Wynniatt nothing of her private affairs. She had, however, happened to mention some friends living at Brighton, and the landlady concluded that her non-appearance was due to her having gone to see them. Not until Saturday morning did Mrs. Wynniatt anticipate any ill befalling her, though she consulted her husband as to the necessity of locating Mrs. Munro with a view to informing her of her daughter's non-return. The post on Saturday brought a registered letter for Irene, which Mrs. Wynniatt thought advisable to open. This letter, from Mrs. Munro, contained 30s., and furnished the Wynniatts with her temporary address at Edinburgh. They decided to telegraph to her, but before doing so Mr. Wynniatt chanced to glance at the day's issue of a local newspaper. That organ announced that the previous night a woman's body had been discovered buried on the Crumbles. Mr. and Mrs. Wynniatt went at once to the police station where they communicated the fact of their lodger's absence. Accompanied by her husband, Mrs. Wynniatt visited the mortuary and was shown the remains of the Crumbles victim. She was horrified to see in her the girl who had come to lodge at her house a few days earlier. The face was so badly disfigured by the violence which had killed her that her landlady found recognition difficult, but the clothes which the dead woman had worn were unmistakable, notably the green coat. Who was Irene Munro's murderer, and what had been his motive for the crime?

II

Amongst the many visitors to Eastbourne that summer were a Mrs. Weller, wife of a Lewisham postmaster, and their schoolboy son William. On Friday, August 20, the two decided to picnic on the Crumbles. About 3.30 in the afternoon the thirteen-year-old lad, running along the rough shingle, tripped and almost fell over some object partly buried in it. From youthful curiosity he stopped to investigate, and found a human foot, clad in a black stocking, without any shoe. His mother, apprised of this exciting discovery, was much upset, and immediately took him back to their lodgings. She told the landlady, Mrs. Lamb, who passed on the information to her husband, a carpenter and joiner, when he returned from work at 5.30. Mr. Lamb did not believe for a moment that a body could be buried there, but in order to satisfy Mrs. Weller, he armed himself with a small garden trowel and, accompanied by William Weller, went to the spot. It was then about 7 p.m., and the Daylight Saving Act being in operation, still light. The foot was in the same position. Mr. Lamb removed some of the shingle and disclosed the body of a young woman clad in a green coat with trimmings of imitation black fur. Her black hat was over her face, the brim weighted down by a large stone. When Mr. Lamb lifted the hat, he saw that the face and head were shockingly injured. The fur collar of the coat covered the mouth. With commendable common sense he touched nothing else, replaced the hat, and dispatched the boy Weller to inform the police. Whilst he awaited their arrival, Mr. Lamb looked round for a possible weapon with which the crime might have been committed, and discovered, 2 yards from the body, an iron-stone brick, 32 lb. in weight, covered with three inches of shingle. This was afterwards seen to bear blood-stains. He came across no bag, purse, or money.

Inspector Cunnington, of the Eastbourne County Borough Police, accompanied by a sergeant, a constable, and William Weller, arrived about eight o'clock. He found Mr. Lamb, who showed him the body lying in a hollow of the beach. The shingle covering it was about six inches in depth on the upper part of the body and chest, more shallow over the feet and legs, and towards the extended right leg very shallow. When the inspector uncovered it further, he saw that the woman was lying on her left side, with her right leg and left arm extended, her left leg bent under the right one, and her right arm bent across her chest, so that the hand came underneath the left arm. The body was fully clothed with the exception of the missing shoe from the right foot, but the coat was folded back about six inches from the thigh, exposing it, and the dress and underclothes were even farther up than the coat.

Beyond lowering the latter for the sake of decency, the inspector touched nothing. He left a constable in charge, and bicycled to Pevensey to summon Superintendent Willard, of the East Sussex Police, as the body had been found just outside the Eastbourne police area. Inspector Cunnington also communicated with Dr. Cadman, police surgeon, and returned with him to the spot. The doctor arrived about eleven o'clock, accompanied by a nurse, who took notes. He examined the body, under the light of an acetylene lamp, and formed the impression that the woman had been killed twenty-four hours previously. The body was then taken in an ambulance to the mortuary at Eastbourne Town Hall, where it was undressed. The deceased girl had been wearing the green coat, a grey coat-frock, a blue petticoat, "what is called a camisole, or something of that sort," white calico combinations, buttoning at the back, garters, black stockings, and a black velvet shoe on the left foot. (The right-foot shoe was afterwards found near where the body had been buried.) She was menstruating, and her combinations and a diaper were both stained. The latter was in exact position. The girl's hair was matted with blood. In the pocket of her dress was a small white paper bag which looked as though it had held sweets. The cause of death, it was subsequently agreed by the medical men who examined the body, had been violent blows on the face and head. There were no signs of indecent assault.

III

The local police, realizing early the seriousness and complexity of the case, lost no time in enlisting the help of Scotland Yard. On Saturday (21st) a representative, Chief Inspector Mercer, arrived at Eastbourne, and proceeded to interview all persons likely to throw any light on the crime. Mrs. Wynniatt was unable to give him much information about Irene Munro. She stated that whilst under her roof the girl had been reticent concerning herself, quiet, well conducted, inoffensive, and received no visitors. She was lent no latch-key, so could not have admitted anyone unknown to Mrs. Wynniatt, as the latter or her husband always locked the street door at night. Several letters came for Irene, and it transpired subsequently that she herself had written to various people, intimating her safe arrival at Eastbourne. These included her mother, Mrs. Sinclair, and a girl-friend, Ada Beasley. A letter from Mrs. Sinclair, found at her lodgings, informing Irene that a ring which she thought she had lost had been discovered at Manson

Place, gave the police her London address, and Mrs. Munro's letter to her daughter, which arrived on the Saturday, also furnished them with the mother's whereabouts. The Edinburgh police authorities were communicated with and requested to ask Mrs. Munro to come to Eastbourne to identify the deceased, but the reply received stated that she had gone to Glasgow, and her address there was not known. The Sinclairs, approached by Scotland Yard, declined to visit the mortuary, so matters were temporarily at a deadlock. Ultimately Mrs. Munro was located, and arrived on the Sunday (22nd), but prior to this, at her sister's wish, Mrs. Winter travelled down from London and saw the body. She recognized it immediately as that of her niece, Irene Munro, and stated that she had last seen her alive a week previously after they both saw Mrs. Munro off at Wapping Pier. Mrs. Winter could not account in any way for the tragedy. When they parted the girl had been perfectly well and was apparently looking forward to her holiday.

Early on the Saturday Inspector Mercer visited the scene of the crime. The Crumbles was a stretch of shingle, several miles in length, from Eastbourne to Pevensey Bay, and about a mile in width from the sea to the main road on the north side. There were houses at intervals along each side of this road, but the Crumbles was entirely beach. Sheds and cottages were the nearest dwellings. On account of its comparative solitude it was a favourite resort for courting couples, but pedestrians found it disagreeable because of the roughness underfoot. Locally its reputation was not too good. People known as "the Eastbourne foxes" were alleged to go there to spy in the hope of witnessing some immorality, and then profiting by levying blackmail. The hole where the body had been buried was 700 or more yards distant from the sea, some 4 feet in depth, and in width 14 by 17 feet. It was all shingle at the sides, top, and bottom. Twenty yards away a railway-line crossed the Crumbles. This was often utilized by persons disliking to walk over the shingle, but its main object was as a track for conveying ballast. Men were employed in loading trucks with this, and after their work was finished they would wait in a derelict railway-carriage nearby, used as a hut for meals or a shelter during bad weather, until an engine fetched them. As a rule the engine came about 3.30 each afternoon.

In the course of his inquiries the Scotland Yard representatives interviewed five men who had been working on the Crumbles the day of the murder. After dinner they were sitting in the hut, which had a view towards the railway-line. Two men and a girl passed in front of the hut, coming from the direction of Eastbourne. They were walking between the metals of the four-foot way, the girl and one man together, the other man slightly in the rear. The first man, the shorter of the two, had his arm round the girl's waist, and all three seemed "very jolly and excited." So hilarious in fact were the trio that a suspicion of their sobriety crossed the mind of one eye-witness. The girl looked in at the window of the hut and smiled as she passed. The incident was further impressed upon the memories of all the hut's occupants by the fact that she had been playing with a stray kitten, and the taller of her companions put it down inside the doorway, saying: "Here's a kitten for you." The three walked on in the direction of Pevensey, which was also the same direction as the hole where Irene Munro's body was afterwards found. Between 3.40 and four o'clock the workmen went away on the engine. They saw no other woman pass that afternoon. Some of them noticed that the girl was dark, with good teeth, and wore a black hat, but nothing special about either of the men had struck any of them. The man walking with the girl carried a stick. They thought that he was wearing a blue suit and his associate a grey one. Inspector Mercer took statements from all five, and later they were shown the remains in the mortuary. Each unhesitatingly identified the body of Irene Munro as the girl whom they had seen with the two men on the afternoon of Thursday.

The same day (Saturday, August 21) a post-mortem examination of the body was made in the afternoon by Dr. Adams, surgeon to the County Borough Police. Dr. Cadman was present and assisted, though he stated later that his rôle had been mainly that of a spectator. Dr. Adams found on the right temple, a short distance from the eyebrow, a small wound of a lacerated character, an irregular penetrating wound on the lip, and to the left of the lip a smaller wound. There was a fracture of the upper and lower jaws, the upper jaw being broken inwards, two teeth missing, and two others forced in. Great violence must have been applied to cause these injuries. There were additional wounds on the left cheek, extending to the temple and beyond the ear. The organs were healthy, the body being that of a well-nourished, strongly made, muscular girl. Half-way up the inside of the right thigh there was a small scratch. The girl was not a virgin, though there were no active signs of pregnancy. The cause of death was shock, following unconsciousness produced by an injury to the left side of the head. The fracture of both jaws and the missing teeth and injured lip were due to a blow from some sharp instrument, possibly a stick with a point. Dr. Adams was of opinion that more than one blow might have been struck before the iron-stone brick completed the fatal injuries. He formed the view that the body had been moved after death in order to facilitate the hasty burial.

IV

Late on Saturday evening the following statement was issued by the police to the press:

> Deceased is Irene Munro, aged between 20 and 25. She described herself as a typist. She has been working in Oxford Street, London, and has resided in Queen's Gate, London.
> The police are satisfied that it is a clear case of murder,

and are endeavouring to trace two men who passed along
the railway-line across the Crumbles towards Pevensey
between 3 and 4 p.m. on Thursday, and also the owner
of a nearly full-grown sandy kitten which had been left
at a hut on the Crumbles.

After Mrs. Munro had arrived at Eastbourne and identified her daughter's body, a second police statement was
published in the press:

> The police have interviewed the mother of the deceased
> girl, Irene Munro, who was eighteen years of age. Her
> movements during Monday, Tuesday, and Wednesday
> have been traced.
> At 4 p.m. on Thursday she was seen walking along
> Seaside past 393 Seaside, where she was residing. She
> was with two fairly tall young men dressed in grey suits
> of herring-bone pattern.
> Just prior to this she had come out of the house and
> had turned towards Eastbourne, apparently to meet these
> two men, neither of whom were wearing hats. Almost
> immediately afterwards she came back and walked
> towards the Crumbles, the three being in conversation
> together.
> The deceased always carried a faded blue silk hand-
> bag, about 9 inches long and 6 inches wide, with a plain
> white metal snap fastening. The bag had a handle which
> passed over the arm, the handle being made of the same
> material as the bag.
> She habitually wore a 9-carat gold ring with a round
> cluster of four, five, or perhaps six small brilliant white
> stones. She is believed to have had between £2 and
> £2 10s. in her possession on Thursday morning. The bag,
> ring, and money cannot be found.
> The police are anxious to trace these articles (which
> can be identified), and also the two men described.

Two of these clues—the sandy kitten and the missing

ring—proved abortive. The kitten was a stray, wandering about the neighbourhood, and Irene Munro had not brought the ring with her to Eastbourne. Mrs. Munro stated that in the girl's last letter to her, written on the morning of the day on which she met her death, she had explained that her holiday expenses were considerable, reducing her finances to about 55s., and asked her mother to send her some money. If robbery had been the motive for killing her, her murderer must have been greatly disappointed at the contents of her bag. Three days after the murder a bunch of keys, identified as Irene Munro's, which she kept in this bag, were found by an Eastbourne holiday-maker not far from the scene of the crime. The police inclined to the theory that her assailant had thrown them away after appropriating the bag and its other contents.

The murder, taking place at the height of the holiday season, aroused an enormous amount of excitement and speculation in Eastbourne. The place was full of rumours. People alleged that they had seen Irene Munro having tea with a man in a tea-garden, or sitting opposite to another man in a local railway-train, or between two men in a motor late on the Thursday night. There proved to be nothing in these stories, but they did not make the task of the police any easier. A mysterious black fluid taken from the girl's stomach was found, after analysis, to be harmless, and her supposed "diary," which Mrs. Wynniatt saw her writing up, resolved itself into a commonplace book in which she jotted down items that chanced to interest or amuse her. Everything was done to endeavour to identify her as a girl seen with a man or two men prior to her death. Her pictures were shown on the screen at local cinemas, and a dummy figure, dressed in her clothes, with the head of the dead girl superimposed on it, was photographed and given wide publicity. Bloodhounds were taken to the scene of the murder, without any result, and at a spiritualistic séance held on the Crumbles Irene herself, alleged to be speaking through a medium, proved excessively disappointing and unhelpful in the matter of solving the riddle of her own death.

Chief Inspector Mercer instituted searching inquiries into the victim's antecedents, character, and circumstances. It appeared that Irene Munro was born at Brighton on November 23, 1902, being within three months of her eighteenth birthday when she met her death. She looked much more than her actual age, people usually taking her for about twenty-five. When she was six she moved to London with her widowed mother. Irene received her education at the William Street Central Girls' School, Hammersmith Road, where she also learned shorthand and typewriting. For more than a year she had been employed by the firm of Messrs. Maxwell & Wright, underwriters, Regent Street. Entering their service as a junior employee, she worked her way up gradually until she became confidential typist to Mr. Maxwell, at a salary of £2 7s. 6d. a week. He stated that he had no fault to find with the manner in which she fulfilled her duties, and gave her an excellent character. Mrs. Sinclair did the same, whilst her mother described her as quiet, reserved, fond of reading, neat, but not extravagant in her dress or personal habits, and all three thought it most unlikely that she would have gone of her own accord with a strange man to a place like the Crumbles. Another side to her nature was, however, revealed by certain girl-acquaintances of Irene Munro. One of these declared that she had been extremely attractive to the opposite sex, and in the habit of boasting about "picking up" unknown male admirers, who took her to expensive restaurants and entertainments and gave her costly presents. When the police came to investigate her home surroundings, all that could be found to substantiate these allegations were certain letters signed "Louis," written in more or less amorous terms, and a gift of a handbag. This was the missing blue silk one, which Irene told her mother she had bought. The clothing on the dead body was of a cheap quality; the girl had only 8d. in her Post Office savings account; and her few receipted bills showed that she had paid for most of her modest wardrobe by instalments. Her holiday luggage, which Mrs. Wynniatt handed over to the police, consisted of a small green fibre-covered suitcase that had contained two or three inexpensive dresses, some cheap beads and brooches, poor underclothing, and valueless personal possessions such as her Bible and dressing-jacket. She gave her mother 13s. weekly towards her board, but Mrs. Munro stated that she did not always take this as Irene had to dress herself out of her earnings. Her fellow-workers liked her, and had noticed her devotion to her mother. One of these probably spoke the truth when she said she knew that certain girls were jealous of Irene's pretty face and smart appearance. No evidence was ever forthcoming to show that she had made money by immorality, though she had undoubtedly deceived her mother as to certain engagements and visits to the theatre with men friends. Mrs. Munro stated at the trial that she only learned after the girl's death that she had been acquainted with someone named Louis, and she did not know of anybody whom Irene called "uncle." The police did not show her the letters discovered amongst her daughter's possessions.

Irene's alleged indiscretions speedily found their way into print. After the revelations of her contemporaries, the popular theory to account for her violent death was that some man known to her in London had followed her to Eastbourne, or met her there by appointment, and a quarrel with him had resulted in the crime. Disappointed lust, or the act of a sexual maniac, was also advanced as explaining the extreme violence used by the murderer, but despite the police vigilance and investigations no arrest was made.

v

On Monday, August 23, the inquest on the body of Irene Munro was opened at Eastbourne Town Hall by

Mr. G. Vere Benson, the East Sussex coroner. When instructing the jury to view the body, he asked them to note particularly the injuries the girl had received. The case he described as one of "very brutal and peculiar murder." It would be impossible to finish the inquest that day, but he hoped to call evidence which would justify his issuing an order for the burial of the body.

Mrs. Munro, the first witness, stated that she had seen the body in the mortuary and identified it as her daughter's. She gave particulars of her age and occupation, and said that she had last seen her on the previous Saturday week. She knew that deceased was going to Eastbourne. She had not been there before. The discovery of the foot by William Weller, and the uncovering of the body in the shingle by Mr. Lamb, were described by both these witnesses. Inspector Cunnington gave evidence of being summoned to the Crumbles on the Friday night about eight o'clock, and of the body being examined by Dr. Cadman. Dr. Adams stated that on the following day he had made a post-mortem examination of the remains and was satisfied as to the cause of death. The Coroner then adjourned the inquest for a fortnight.

On August 25 Dr. Elworthy, pathologist to the West London Hospital, went by the request of the Home Office authorities to Eastbourne for the purpose of making a further examination of the body of Irene Munro. He knew from Dr. Adams's previous examination what the injuries were, and agreed with his conclusions entirely. He formed the same opinion as to the cause of death, i.e., shock, following on blows to the jaws, head, and face, and thought the iron-stone brick had been the principal weapon employed. If the girl were knocked down and stunned and her body dragged a short distance, that would account for the disarrangement of her clothing and the loss of one shoe. Both Dr. Adams and Dr. Elworthy were in accord that when the body was found Irene Munro had been dead a much longer time than that suggested by Dr. Cadman. The

conditions were consistent with her having been killed
between 3.30 and 5.30 on the Thursday afternoon.

The funeral was originally fixed for Wednesday, August
25, but had to be postponed to allow of the second post-
mortem examination. It took place the following day
instead. Exactly a week after her murder the remains of
Irene Munro were buried in Langney Cemetery, Eastbourne, on Thursday morning, August 26. The plate on
the coffin bore merely her name and age, the date of her
death, and the words "Thy Will be done." Her uncle,
Mr. Louttitt, and her friend Ada Beasley were the principal
mourners. Her mother sent a wreath, but was not present.
The police were reticent, nevertheless a tentative arrest had
been made in the case two days earlier.

VI

During Monday (23rd) a local labourer named Frederick
Wells had gone to the police with an important statement.
He informed them that on the afternoon of Thursday,
August 19, he was in the company of Putland, the young
naval stoker who had noticed a girl, wearing a green coat,
on the beach on Tuesday morning. The two men lived in
adjacent roads—Myrtle Road and Alfrey Road—both leading into Seaside. They met in Seaside about 1.45, just below
the Alexandra Arms. Putland invited his friend to have a
drink with him, and the pair went into another inn, the
Arlington Arms, remaining for a quarter of an hour. When
they emerged, they stood outside the inn for about ten
minutes. On the opposite side of the road a girl and two
men came along, walking in the direction of the Crumbles.
Wells had a good opportunity of seeing them, but stated
that "he never took much notice of the girl." All he could
say about how she was dressed was that she wore a black
hat, turned up at the back, with a transparent brim, a check
skirt, and a black blouse, but he could not swear to these
things. He thought she had a green coat over her arm. Her

hair was dark, and she showed good teeth. Her age, so far as he could judge, was from twenty to twenty-five. She was walking between two men, the shorter of whom Wells had seen about in Eastbourne several times during the preceding fortnight. He was dressed in a blue serge suit and a light cap, and carried a stick, yellow in colour, with a dog's head on the handle. His companion wore a grey suit and a trilby hat. Wells put the ages of both at from twenty-seven to twenty-eight. The three were going along "just ordinarily," and Wells had no particular reason for noticing them, but his attention was drawn to them by Putland's remarking that he had seen them together on the previous day. Wells was temporarily unemployed and Putland on leave, so, both being idle, Wells agreed to Putland's suggestion that they should follow these people. Asked at the trial what his motive was in proposing this to Wells, Putland answered frankly: "Just to pass away the time, and to see what they would do." He took his bicycle home, rejoined Wells, and the two went after the trio who in the meanwhile had passed Wells and were a short distance ahead. At Fort Road, just at the beginning of the Crumbles, they saw them get under a fence some 50 yards from the railway-line crossing the shingle. The girl offered her companions a white paper bag which Wells thought contained sweets. He and Putland continued along Seaside, parallel with the Crumbles, the three people being on one side of the fence and Wells and Putland on the other. They walked up a cinder track that branched off at right angles from the road, and saw a sandy kitten, which Wells had noticed straying about three weeks earlier, being picked up and caressed by the girl. Afterwards she and the two men were proceeding along the railway-line towards the railway-hut. Wells refused to follow them any farther, alleging that he disliked the look of the stick the shorter man carried. Putland and Wells returned to Eastbourne.

The following morning they and a friend named Piper were together in Victoria Place, a road leading on to the

Parade, when Putland and Wells saw the two men both had gone after the day before. They were talking to two girls neither of whom was the girl who had been walking with them the previous afternoon. Early on Monday morning Putland left Eastbourne to rejoin his ship at East Cowes, and Wells, who had had no communication with him since hearing of the Crumbles murder on Sunday forenoon, went to the police later in the day and related what he had witnessed on Thursday. Asked why he had not done so sooner, Wells replied that "he thought he would leave it until next day." He described the two men and the girl as well as he could to Chief Inspector Mercer. On Tuesday (24th) Wells went with the inspector and another police official to the Parade where he saw the same two men, this time talking to three girls. Wells pointed out the shorter man, whom he recognized more than the other, mainly by his walk. As a result, both men were detained by the police and their statements taken.

VII

William Thomas Gray and Jack Alfred Field, the two suspects, were residents of Eastbourne, both out of work, and thoroughly undesirable characters. Gray, the older, was aged twenty-eight, and described himself as a plate-layer, though he added optimistically that he was endeavouring to obtain a post as a cinematograph operator. Born in South Africa, of Scottish parentage, he had come over with the South African Heavy Artillery, during 1915, and served with that force until his discharge in August, 1917. Since then Gray had settled at Eastbourne, marrying a native of the town, a seventeen-year-old girl named Anderson. He received a small disability pension which, just prior to the Crumbles murder, had been reduced to 8s. a week. His wife worked as a daily servant, and Gray, unemployed for twelve months, spent his enforced leisure in lounging about the beach or Parade, talking to young women, or visiting

public-houses and places of amusement. Hitherto he had
not actually been in the hands of the Eastbourne police for
any offence, but he was known to them as a worthless
individual, notorious for his relations with the opposite
sex. He was completely illiterate, admitting himself that
he could neither read nor write.

Field, the younger man, was a lad of nineteen or twenty,
better educated and better equipped mentally. He may, as
Mr. Edward Marjoribanks suggests in his brief account of
the case in the *Life of Sir Edward Marshall Hall*, have been
under Gray's influence, but on his own belated admission
it was Field who concocted the story designed to save their
necks when—or even before—suspicion was directed to him
and Gray as Irene Munro's killers. Field had served in the
Navy, being discharged the previous April. He stated that
the reason was given on his discharge papers, which probably meant that he was dismissed the service. He had been
in trouble with the police several times and had previous
convictions. During August, 1920, he was in receipt of
29s. weekly as unemployment benefit. After becoming
acquainted two months previously Field and Gray were
constantly together, sharing a liking for bars, cinemas, seaside flirtations, and the swimming-baths. At the trial Mr.
Justice Avory remarked on the amount of money that both
seemed to have had to squander on entertainment. Field
lived with his mother, grandmother, brother, and sister at
23 Susans Road, Eastbourne, which was near Gray's home
in Longstone Road. His parents were hard-working, respectable people, the father acting as a head waiter in London,
whilst his wife took summer lodgers.

On the morning of August 19 Field and Gray came into
the public bar of the Albemarle, a hotel on the Parade.
The time was just after twelve o'clock. The two barmaids,
Dorothy Ducker and Elsie Finley, had known both as customers for about a fortnight, though they were unacquainted
with their identities or surnames, addressing them respectively as "Billy" and "Jack." Gray was always clad in a

grey suit and a trilby hat, and Field in a dark suit, dark cap, and brown shoes. Up to the morning of the 19th Miss Ducker had never seen Gray attired any differently, but she had noticed Field wearing a straw hat. She had comparatively little to do with Field, but Gray joked with her and pressed unwelcome attentions upon her. Although he used to complain of being hard up, he suggested repeatedly that she should go with him to cinemas. These invitations were invariably declined. On the 19th, as the two were leaving the bar about 1 p.m., after laughing and jesting with Miss Ducker, and enjoying several glasses of bitter each, Gray asked her if she had any biscuits. She told him that he would not want biscuits when he was just going home to his lunch, but Gray explained that he meant biscuits for his dog. She inquired where the dog was, whereupon Gray held up the handle of a walking-stick. As well as Miss Ducker could remember, it had a bulldog's head on it, but she did not see it sufficiently long to be able to describe it more fully. The pair came back about two o'clock and drank a glass of bitter apiece. Undeterred by previous snubs, Gray proposed a visit to a picture-house that afternoon, which Miss Ducker promptly refused. They then called for a cheaper variety of beer, and asked if they could have a drink for nothing. Miss Ducker answered, "No, of course not," whereupon Gray again repeated his invitation to the cinema. Miss Ducker declined decisively, and Gray said: "Very well, if you wait till the evening we shall have more money by then." The barmaid asked whether they were hard up again, and Gray replied that she knew that he was out of work and his pension small. He mentioned that he and Field would return about 6.30, and proposed that Miss Ducker should go with them to the evening performance at the Hippodrome. She refused as usual, and they went away, the time being 2.30. Both were dressed as they had been when they were in the bar during the forenoon. The Albemarle had two bars, a public and a private one. At 6.30 the same evening Miss Ducker was sitting in the private bar, ready to go out. It was her night off duty, and she had decided to go to the first house at the Hippodrome, a short distance away. Field and Gray came into the public bar and asked Miss Finley, the other barmaid, where her colleague was. The three then came round to the private bar, and Gray invited both girls to have something to drink. Each accepted, Miss Ducker choosing port wine and Miss Finley whisky and soda. The two men drank bottled beer, a thing Miss Ducker had never known them to have before. Gray paid for all the drinks. He and Field were also smoking expensive cigarettes, and offered the box to both barmaids. Miss Ducker could not remember the make, but "it was a jolly good cigarette." Miss Finley, accustomed to seeing these men smoking a much cheaper kind of tobacco, remarked on the brand, whereupon Field replied: "We can have a good cigarette sometimes if we want to." Gray asked Miss Ducker if she were going with him and Field to the Hippodrome, but she again said no.

A change in Gray's appearance had immediately struck Miss Ducker, and she told him that he looked dirty. He was wearing a dark suit and cap, and his boots were, to quote Miss Ducker's expression, "filthy dirty." His explanation was that when on the beach that afternoon Field had pushed him into the water, and as his clothes were not dry by six o'clock he had had to change them. Miss Ducker had never seen him thus attired before, or known him to change his garments in the course of the day. Field heard Gray's answer, but made no comment beyond a smile. Miss Ducker then went off for her evening's amusement, leaving both men in the Albemarle. She was at the Hippodrome for about two hours—from 7 till 9 p.m.—and during the performance noticed that Field and Gray had come in and were sitting about four seats behind her. In the interval she looked round and saw that they had gone out.

The two went to the bar, where Field treated Gray and one of the attendants, a man named MacMullen, to a drink each. He then paid back a sum of 2s. which he had borrowed from MacMullen three months previously. MacMullen was surprised at receiving his money, and asked the (in the circumstances) maladroit question: "Well, have you been setting about somebody?" Field also repaid 7s. to a man called Burton who was at the Hippodrome that night, the transaction being witnessed by another attendant who noticed that Field was smoking Turkish cigarettes. Burton thought both Field and Gray slightly the worse for drink. After the performance was over, they went back to the Albemarle and had more beer, treating one or two men whom they met in the bar, and remaining until 10.30 p.m.

Between eight and nine o'clock Field and Gray left the Hippodrome. At the corner of St. John's Road they accosted a girl whom they saw posting a letter. The young woman, Hilda Maud Baxter, was employed as a scullery-maid at a house called Ravenhurst, and this brief expedition to the pillar-box was her first outing on the 19th. The two men wished her good evening, and one of them asked if they might walk home with her. She agreed, and parted from them at the gate of Ravenhurst without learning their names. Three days later (Sunday, August 22) she encountered them again near the Wish Tower. The three sat on a seat and talked. Miss Baxter said that she was leaving Eastbourne the following Saturday to return to her home at Colchester, and gave as her reason for being glad to go that there had been one murder at Eastbourne and "she was afraid of getting murdered herself." Gray replied: "It is not Eastbourne. It is the people who come from London." When they parted, he suggested a further meeting, and appointed 3.30 on Monday afternoon at St. John's Road. The trio duly met then, and went up to the golf-links where, after picking some blackberries, they sat on a bank. Gray told Miss Baxter that he and Field were brothers named Billy and Jack White, and that they lived near the Hippodrome. Following a diet of blackberries, Miss Baxter went home to tea, but she agreed to meet the two men again the same evening about seven o'clock. They took a walk along the sea front in the Beachy Head direction and sat on the last seat. The conversation turned upon the previous Thursday, the day of the Crumbles murder, and Gray said that during the afternoon he and Field had been to Pevensey. He went into certain details, notably as to times, as though endeavouring to impress the incidents on Miss Baxter's memory. They asked her if she had visited the place, and she replied that she had not. Gray carried a copy of the special edition of the *Eastbourne Gazette* and, appearing to read from it, said that the police were looking for two men in grey suits, and also repeated the description of Irene Munro's missing bag and ring. He saw Miss Baxter home as far as the corner of her road, and arranged to meet her again on the following night (Tuesday), but the appointment was never kept. Field and Gray were unavoidably detained by the police, and Miss Baxter, after an interview with an official, refused to see them when they came to the house following their release. On the whole she was fortunate to escape with nothing more serious than the loss of her watch. Under pretence of having it repaired, Gray borrowed it from her, and it was afterwards found at his house, thus proving him a petty thief. Miss Baxter herself repudiated Field's story that the watch had been a gift.

VIII

Field and Gray were taken by Detective-Inspector Wells, of the Eastbourne County Borough Police, to Latimer Road Police Station. On the way neither spoke. In the inspector's office Wells said that they would wonder why they had been brought there, and Field replied: "We have been expecting this, as we both wear grey suits." Gray, who heard the answer, made no observation. The official next said that he would not ask them anything, but would communicate with Chief Inspector Mercer. The pair were then taken to the Central Police Station at the Town Hall, where the Scotland Yard detective interviewed both. Whilst waiting for him,

Field and Gray, under the charge of a constable, were left in a small room, 16 feet 5 inches long and 10 feet 6 inches wide. Field afterwards alleged that a certain conversation took place between him and Gray, but it was proved that this could not have been so without the policeman over-hearing. He stated that two very brief remarks were all that was said by either man.

Chief Inspector Mercer interviewed each separately. He told Field, to whom he spoke first, that he had been asked to come to the police station because it was said that he was crossing the line on the Crumbles near the two huts with another man and a woman about 3 p.m. on Thursday, August 19. The inspector added that Field was to take plenty of time and think carefully before making any state-ment. He was not compelled to say anything unless he liked, but any explanation he cared to give as to where he was on that day would be taken down. These words headed Field's subsequent statement. He gave his name as Jack Alfred Field, his age as nineteen, added that he was of no occupa-tion, had been recently discharged from the Navy, and lived at 23 Susans Road, Eastbourne. After he had read over his statement, Field signed it and said it was correct.

Accounting for his movements on August 19, Field said that from 10.30 a.m. till 1 p.m. he and Gray were sitting on the sea-front. He said that he went home to dinner at one, leaving again about 2 p.m., and meeting Gray at his house in Longstone Road about five minutes later. He and Gray walked straight along Seaside, past the Crumbles, to Peven-sey Bay. At Pevensey Castle they sat down on the castle green, and whilst there Miss Baxter passed them. Field gave her name and address, said that Gray spoke to her, and she stayed with them till four o'clock. The three walked back together the same way that Field and Gray had come, arriving at Leaf Hall about 5 p.m. They had ices at a restaurant called the Criterion, and at 5.30 Field and Gray left Miss Baxter and went to Gray's house where they played cards till 6.15. Field left when Mrs. Gray came in,

and returned to his own home for tea. He called for Gray
again about 6.30 or 6.45, and they went to the Hippodrome,
arriving about 7 p.m. About nine they visited the Albemarle and remained till ten o'clock. They then returned to
the Hippodrome, leaving about eleven o'clock, when Field
went home to bed. The next day (Friday, 20th) was spent
mostly on the sea-front, or in visiting picture-houses. Field
stated that on the 19th he was wearing a grey double-
breasted coat, grey flannel trousers, and a straw hat. He
denied that he carried a stick, or that he crossed the
Crumbles on Thursday or Friday. He had no cat in his
possession either day.

This statement, in addition to being a tissue of untruths
and misrepresentations, contained several highly important
omissions. Field made no mention of his and Gray's calls
at the Albemarle on the 19th before and after lunch, or at
6.30, but gave the impression that their visit in the late
evening was the first time they had been there that day.
He did not say in his statement that after lunch he and
Gray mounted a bus which took them to the Archery, a fact
mentioned by Gray in his statement, and subsequently corroborated by a witness who knew both men. He did not
refer to walking with or talking to any girl, though, as
Mr. Justice Avory remarked in his summing up, there was
no reason why he should have concealed the fact unless
she were the deceased one, Irene Munro. Field also stated
that on Thursday, at midday, he went home to dinner,
whereas he had gone to a restaurant in Langney Road for
this.

Gray's statement, taken from him after he had received
a similar caution to Field's, followed much the same lines
as the latter's. He stated that on the 19th he left his house
at 10 a.m. and went straight to the sea-front, where he
met Field. They stayed there, listening to the band, till
1 p.m., and then walked back together to Field's house,
where Gray went home. They met again soon after two, at
the corner of Bourne Street and Longstone Road, and

walked to Leaf Hall where they took a bus to the Archery. There they alighted and went at once down Pevensey road to Pevensey Castle. They reached the Castle about 3.30 or 3.45, and sat on the castle green. Here they met "a lady friend whose name was Maud." Gray alleged that he did not know her surname, but knew her at Colchester when he was stationed there. She was in service at a house in St. John's Road, Eastbourne, but though she told him the name, Gray had forgotten it. The meeting at Pevensey was an accidental one. He introduced her to Field, and they all returned together to Eastbourne. Gray stated that they walked to the Archery, and there took a bus to Leaf Hall. He asked the driver the time and was told that it was 5.15. At Field's suggestion they had ices at a small shop after leaving the bus. He and Gray then went to Gray's house which they reached "about ten past six." They stayed there for an hour and then walked to the Albion Hotel, and from this went to the Hippodrome. Here they remained from 7.30 till nine, and then left the place and walked to the station. Returning to the Albion, they had another drink and left about 9.30. Field, Gray and two men whom they met in the Albion walked together to Victoria Place where they parted, Gray returning with Field as far as his house and then going on to his own. He detailed his movements on Friday much as Field had done, mentioning visits to two picture-houses. Gray denied that he had ever met "the young lady whose photograph is in the *Daily Mirror* of August 23" (Irene Munro), or that he had gone across the Crumbles on the 19th or the 20th. He further added that, although a resident in Eastbourne for three years, he "had never been across there in my life." Neither he nor Field had had a cat in his possession on Thursday or Friday. On these days he was dressed in navy blue, a suit which he had been wearing for about two weeks previously, and on Thursday he wore a trilby hat. He admitted to the ownership of a grey suit at home.

Gray's statement was as inaccurate as Field's. He, too,

omitted the essential events, such as the two early visits to the Albemarle on the 19th, and either deliberately, or by mistake, as they were adjoining, confused the name of the hotel with that of its neighbour, the Albion. Certain times which he gave did not tally with Field's, though the main outlines of their stories were similar. No charge was then made against either, but they were told that they would be detained whilst their statements were investigated. The following day (25th) the men from the railway-hut attended an identification parade, but failed to pick out either man as the companion of the girl they had seen on the 19th.

Miss Baxter was interviewed by the police and immediately denied the story of Field and Gray that she had been with both at Pevensey on the afternoon of August 19. Her statement that she was not out of the house all day until she went to the post that evening was corroborated by her fellow-servants, two sisters-in-law named Hawes, who testified to the fact that the three of them had had tea together at Ravenhurst during the material time. Police officials also searched Field's house and took possession of a stick ornamented with a dog's head, a grey jacket, a light waistcoat, a khaki cap, and a straw hat. At Gray's house a grey suit was found, and two trilby hats. None of these articles bore blood-stains, nor was any of Irene Munro's missing property found at either home. When shown the stick on the 25th by Inspector Mercer, Field acknowledged that it was his, but denied that he had had it with him on the 19th. Informed that Miss Baxter had stated that she was not with them at Pevensey, Field replied that "he must have been mistaken as to the young lady," but still swore that he had been there. When Gray was told the same and informed that he would be further detained, he said nothing.

On the 26th, after two days' detention, the police officials were obliged to release Field and Gray without any charge being made against either, but the authorities continued to amass evidence which tended to prove that both men had

certainly been in the company of Irene Munro on the afternoon of the day she met her death. A conductor named
George Blackmer, employed by the Eastbourne Motor-bus
Corporation, stated that he was due to commence duty at
3.6 p.m. on the 19th. Near Firle Road he boarded an
omnibus scheduled to arrive at the depot beside the Archery
at 2.45. Whilst standing on the platform, a piece of paper
struck him, but on looking round he could not see who had
thrown it. When passengers alighted at the Archery, Blackmer got off and saw Field and Gray, with whom he had
been acquainted for some months, also leaving the vehicle
from the upper deck. He was wearing a new uniform
recently served out to him, and Field accused him of being
too proud to speak to Gray and himself on this account.
Blackmer laughingly denied the accusation, and after a few
seconds' conversation with both, moved away to talk to the
driver of the bus. He was going towards the depot when
he chanced to look round and saw a girl crossing the road
from the bus shelter. She was walking to where Field and
Gray were standing, and as she advanced she called out:
"Hullo, Jack!" Blackmer was not a good judge of distance.
He stated that the girl was 100 feet away from him when
he saw her and heard her voice, but it was subsequently
proved to have been a much shorter space. He did not
notice whether she wore a coat, but thought she carried a
small black handbag, and was wearing a black hat and a
blue dress. He studied her face sufficiently to recognize later
a strong likeness between her and certain photographs of
Irene Munro, though he would not swear that she was the
girl he had seen. Field and Gray he could not be mistaken
about, and he was positive that both wore grey suits.

Farther along Seaside, a little beyond the Archery, some
new houses were in process of erection. On the 19th a
plasterer's labourer named Charles Gordon Dyer was working there. Between 2.30 and 3 p.m. he was in front of the
houses, mixing up some mortar, when three people passed,
walking in a row, going towards the Crumbles. One of the

men Dyer recognized as Gray. He was nearest to Dyer, and the other man, whom Dyer did not know, was walking arm-in-arm with a girl. Dyer was no doubt ruffled at having to work on a hot August afternoon whilst other less deserving cases idled and enjoyed themselves. He pointed out Gray to his workmate, Jupp, remarking that as a married man Gray ought to be ashamed to go about with girls. Jupp rejoined that Gray was not the only one who did so, whereupon Dyer said that Gray made his wife go out to work to keep him. Gray was attired in a light grey suit and trilby hat, and Dyer thought that the other man was dressed similarly, but he did not see him well or take much notice of him. Jupp barely glanced at the trio, and could not recognize either of the men subsequently. He was not particularly interested in the incident, though he corroborated Dyer as to the details and Dyer's observations. He remembered the date by a circus being in Eastbourne near to where he and Dyer were working, and giving its last performances on August 19. He recollected that one man was taller than the other, but noticed nothing about the girl or what she was wearing.

Early on Saturday (August 21) the posters outside the local newsagents had published the finding of a woman's body on the Crumbles. Within a couple of hours of this announcement Field and Gray were at a military camp some miles from Eastbourne, making inquiries about enlisting in the Army. They did not give any names. Gray told Sergeant Hubble, who interviewed both, that he was out of work and his pension had been reduced. Field said nothing. The recruiting-sergeant was away for the day, and neither man adopted a suggestion that they should go to Bexhill where, in the event of their being accepted by the Army authorities, their railway-fares would be refunded. This significant episode found no place in the statements both made to Inspector Mercer.

Immediately after their temporary detention and release Field and Gray, totally unabashed, reappeared in their old haunts. Near the Pier Hotel they met an acquaintance named Grayling. Gray informed him that he and Field had been "locked up," and when Grayling inquired the reason, added "as regards the Crumbles turn-out." Grayling said that this was surprising and offered the two men a drink. The three went into the hotel, and whilst drinking together Field remarked to Grayling: "We were down that way in the afternoon with a girl, but, since, the young girl has come forward to prove our statement that we were down there the same day with her." On coming out of the hotel Field left Gray and Grayling, and Gray, referring to Field, said: "Yes, I shall be getting into trouble with him before long."

Outside the Albemarle, later in the day, Field and Gray met Miss Ducker, to whom they boasted of their prison experiences. She at once realized that the "Jack and Billy" who had been her customers were also the "Field and Gray" about whom the police had come making inquiries. No reference was then made to the events of the previous Thursday, though the same evening the two men reminded Miss Ducker that they had been at the Hippodrome that night. She commented upon Gray's shabby appearance, and he told her that the police still had possession of his suit. Field added that they also had his cap and stick, but the incident of the stick with the dog's head did not recur to Miss Ducker's memory until some time afterwards. Her last sight of Gray as a customer was one night about a week later. He was sitting in the private bar and Miss Ducker was serving patrons in the public one. One of these asked her if she had seen "the latest about the murder." A sailor had come forward with certain information. Miss Ducker took the paper to Gray, accompanied by the same question. He answered that he had been looking for it all night, snatched the paper from her, ostensibly read the news, and went out. She never saw him again a free man.

IX

On Monday, August 23, William Putland had caught the 8.28 a.m. train from Eastbourne to return to his ship at East Cowes. At the station he bought a picture paper in which he read an account of the Crumbles murder. He had heard the previous Saturday that a body had been found on the Crumbles, but was not much interested. His attention was now attracted by a portrait of Irene Munro, wearing a hat and coat. The face struck him by its likeness to the girl whom he had seen on the beach on Tuesday morning, with two men on Wednesday afternoon, and again on Thursday in their company. Four days after rejoining his ship Putland mentioned the matter to another sailor, and on August 30 his commanding officer sent for him and took a statement from him. This was duly forwarded to the police authorities at Eastbourne, and subsequently Putland was asked to return there. On September 2 Chief Inspector Mercer interviewed him, and on Saturday, September 4, by his instructions, Putland walked along the Parade. He noticed two men drinking tea at a coffee-stall, and recognized the shorter man as the one he had seen on Wednesday and Thursday with the girl and another man. On this occasion he was wearing a trilby hat, whereas on the Thursday he had worn a soft cap. The other man was dressed differently from the way the shorter man's companion had been, and now wore a cap. Putland could not identify him. He pointed out the first man to the police. Shown a number of caps, Putland picked out one as identical with the cap the shorter man had worn on the Thursday, and he also selected from a pile of coats a green one as similar to the coat he had seen the girl wearing on three occasions. Inspector Mercer did not tell him that Wells had made a statement and also identified one of the men.

At seven o'clock on the evening of September 4 Chief Inspector Mercer accosted Field outside his home in Susans Road. He told Field that he would have to accompany him again to the police station and the reason would be ex-plained when they reached it. Field replied: "I have been up there every day," and added, after they had walked some distance and the inspector proposed hailing a cab: "All right, and then you can give me my things." At the Town Hall Inspector Mercer said: "You will be charged with being concerned with Gray in the wilful murder of Miss Munro at the Crumbles on August 19. A sailor named Putland identified you this afternoon when you were at the coffee-stall on the beach as a man he saw with her there at 3 p.m. on the 19th." Field, when cautioned in the usual way, asked if he could see the sailor. He was told that he would have an opportunity of doing so, and then said: "You have had my statement and you are no man not to believe it. I kept quiet before, but I shall not this time. I have told you the truth."

At 8.15 the same evening Chief Inspector Mercer and Inspector Wells saw Gray in Seaside. The occasion was noteworthy for the fact that Gray for once happened to be walking with his wife instead of another woman. Inspector Wells spoke to Gray, telling him that he would have to accompany him to the police station. Gray's reply was: "All right." He was taken in a cab to the Town Hall, where Inspector Wells said: "You are to be charged with being concerned with Jack Field in the wilful murder of Miss Munro on the Crumbles on August 19. A sailor has identi-fied Field as being with her there on the 19th, and you say in your statement you were with him that afternoon, but the sailor did not identify you." After being cautioned, Gray said: "I spoke the honest truth the other day. If I did not, may I be struck dead. I wish I had never come to England."

The adjourned inquest on Irene Munro was resumed on September 6, and after several hearings terminated in a verdict of "Wilful murder" against both Field and Gray. When returning their verdict, the jury added that in their opinion the murder was committed during the afternoon of August 19. The proceedings before the Magistrates ultimately ended with a similar finding. Both men, who pleaded "Not guilty," were committed for trial at the next local assizes. During the time between their arrest and the hearing of the case, they were in separate cells at Maidstone Prison. Whilst there, Gray made futile attempts to persuade a prisoner on remand to assist him in establishing an alibi for the afternoon of the 19th. He also entered into conversation on the subject of the murder with a convict serving a sentence for theft. The evidence of these two men, both unbiased and unbribed, told heavily against Gray at his trial.

X

The trial of Field and Gray for the murder of Irene Munro took place before Mr. Justice Avory at the County Hall, Lewes, in December, 1920. It opened on Monday, the 13th of the month, and lasted for five days. Mr. C. F. Gill, K.C. (later Sir Charles Gill), Mr. Curtis Bennett, K.C. (later Sir Henry Curtis Bennett), and Mr. Cecil Whiteley appeared for the Crown. The finances for the defence were provided by the proprietors of *John Bull*. Field was defended by Mr. J. D. Cassels (later Mr. Justice Cassels), and Mr. G. P. Robinson; Gray by Sir Edward Marshall Hall, K.C., and Mr. John Flowers. The previous month Marshall Hall had secured an acquittal for his client Harold Greenwood at Carmarthen Assizes on a charge of poisoning his first wife, but he was not destined to score a similar triumph in the Crumbles trial.

The Crown case was more or less straightforward. Several witnesses, although they differed in regard to details such as the girl's dress, had practically identified Irene Munro as the young woman seen with two men at or near the spot where her body was afterwards found, and the identity of her companions was clearly established by people who knew Field and Gray personally. The accused could produce no water-tight alibi, and the lines which the defence proposed to follow were in the nature of a forlorn hope. The medical opinions as to the time when Irene Munro met her death had been conflicting. Dr. Cadman placed this as twenty-four hours before he saw the body, i.e., 11 p.m. on the Thursday night. The other two doctors both concurred in the view that she was killed during the afternoon of the 19th, between 3.30 and 5.30 p.m. If the murder had been committed at night, Field and Gray could call witnesses to prove that they were in Eastbourne then, either at the Hippodrome, the Albemarle, or their own homes, but if in the afternoon, they were unable to produce a single person who had seen them, as their statements alleged, at Pevensey or elsewhere during the material time.

With the exception of Mrs. Wynniatt, who did not see her go out on the 19th, but only surmised from her movements that she had done so, it is curious that during the day she met her death no woman noticed Irene Munro sufficiently to recollect and identify her. All the witnesses— Rogers, Verrall, Blackmer, Dyer, Jupp, Putland, Wells, and the workers from the railway-hut—were men. Consequently there was a considerable diversity of opinion amongst these as to how she was dressed, a fact of which the defence was not slow to take advantage. A further point in favour of the accused, which Marshall Hall stressed in his concluding speech for Gray, was that evidence had been called to show that Irene Munro was a girl of a certain refinement, with particular tastes, and most unlikely to associate with two shabby, out-of-work men like the accused. This was possible in a measure, but, as the Judge pointed out during the course of his summing up, neither prisoner appeared at his best when in the dock. The girl was, unfortunately for herself, prone to let strangers make her acquaintance, and Field and Gray quite obviously made a habit of starting temporary friendships with unknown young women, as evidenced by the ease with which they insinuated themselves into the company of Miss Baxter.

After both prisoners had pleaded "Not guilty" to the

indictment, Mr. Gill opened the case for the Crown. He described the relative positions of Field and Gray, both ex-service men, out of work, and living near to each other in Eastbourne. He then referred to Irene Munro, her social status, her employment, age, and the fact that on August 16 she had gone to Eastbourne for a fortnight's holiday. During the afternoon of the 19th she left her lodgings at Mrs. Wynniatt's and never returned. The discovery of her body next day on the Crumbles, the two-mile stretch of shingle which ran between Eastbourne and Pevensey Bay, was retold, and the injuries revealed at the post-mortem detailed. The case for the prosecution, Mr. Gill stated, was that on the afternoon of August 19 the two accused met Irene Munro close to her lodgings and accompanied her to the place where she was subsequently murdered. They had been with her at the time of her death, which amounted to saying that they were the persons who inflicted the violence which resulted in it. The episodes at the Albemarle were gone into, the clothes worn by both men, the incident of the stick bearing a dog's head, the meeting of Blackmer with the prisoners outside the Archery Tavern, and his seeing a girl come and speak to them, whom he identified by her photographs as Irene Munro. The additional statements by Dyer, Jupp, Putland, Wells, and the five men in the railway-hut were touched upon. The latter were the last people who saw the girl alive. The time could be proved as being soon after 3.30 in the afternoon.

Dealing with the actual crime, Mr. Gill explained that nothing could be said as to how the murder happened. The girl might have objected to some suggestion made to her, and been struck down in a fit of rage. Realizing that they must silence her for good, the heavy stone was probably taken up and dropped on her face, causing the fatal injuries. Burial in the shingle followed, and the body might have been dragged some distance, thus accounting for the missing shoe and the disarrangement of the clothing.

Counsel next described the actions of the accused for

the rest of the day and the two following. At 6.30 on the evening of Thursday they were once more in the bar of the Albemarle, spending money freely. They treated the two barmaids to a drink each and were smoking expensive cigarettes. Next day they were about in Eastbourne and visited a couple of cinemas. Early on the Saturday the news of the body being found on the Crumbles was announced and caused a great sensation. At 10.30 the same morning the prisoners visited a military camp two miles out of Eastbourne and endeavoured to enlist. The suggestion of the prosecution was that they anticipated arrest and were preparing a story which might exonerate them. They knew that the time to be accounted for was the afternoon of Thursday. Counsel then referred to the statements both men made when detained by Inspector Mercer and to the fact that their stories tallied as to where they were and whom they were with, i.e., at Pevensey Castle, in the company of 'Miss Baxter. If the jury were satisfied that this tale was not only false, but concocted, that had an important bearing on the question of their guilt or innocence. The Crown contended that they had been together before, at the time of, and after, the murder, and whoever identified one, the other was equally proved his companion. If the jury accepted the evidence of these witnesses, the accused had lied about their movements on the day of the crime.

Mr. Gill then dealt with the statements made by two prisoners in Maidstone Gaol, men with whom Gray had held certain conversations. It was for the jury to say whether they could accept such evidence, but he submitted that they could not regard it lightly. In conclusion, counsel said that the important question was whether the two men seen passing the railway-hut with the dead girl were the two men in the dock. If the Crown satisfied the jury upon that, the rest of the evidence was consistent with the accused's guilt, and all their subsequent conduct was consistent with their guilt, especially the fact that, after having an opportunity of considering the matter, they had put forward a concocted and deliberately false statement as to their whereabouts at the time.

The first witnesses called were an architect and a photographer, each of whom produced plans and photographs of certain areas connected with the case. The boy Weller and Mr. Lamb then gave brief evidence as to the finding of the body on the Crumbles. There was no cross-examination of either by Marshall Hall, but on Field's behalf Mr. Cassels asked Mr. Lamb a few questions. The evidence of Inspector Cunnington and Superintendent Willard followed. This closed the first day's proceedings, which had been considerably hindered by the action necessitated by a juror's request for exemption on the ground of ill-health.

At the second day's hearing Dr. Cadman was the first witness called. He described his summons to the Crumbles on the night of the 19th and his examination there of Irene Munro's body. It was cold and *rigor mortis* so well established that he could not move the limbs. Whilst he made his examination, the doctor was sitting on the large iron-stone brick, and not until he had finished his task did he examine the brick and see blood-stains on one side of it. He thought the blow on the jaw was the original one struck. In cross-examination by Mr. Cassels the witness stated that when he first saw the body he formed and advanced the opinion that the girl had been dead approximately from twelve to twenty-four hours. He gave evidence at both the inquest and the police court proceedings, but could not remember whether he stated this fact at either. He now stated that he thought the condition in which he found the body on Friday night consistent with death having taken place on the Thursday afternoon, but refused to commit himself to a positive time, *rigor mortis*, on which he based his first conclusions, being extremely indefinite. It would set in six hours after death. When the witness saw the body again at 2.30 on the afternoon of the next day, it was relaxed to the extent that the arms and legs were down. Beyond the disarrangement of the clothing he saw no signs of any struggle. He examined the body to see whether the girl had been held by the throat or wrists, but noticed nothing to support this view. The small scratch half-way up the inside of the right thigh witness thought had been inflicted during, or just before, the death struggle. He knew on the evening when he first saw the body that the time factor would be a matter of importance in the case. Nothing during the post-mortem examination made by Dr. Adam, at which witness was present, mainly as a spectator, had altered his original opinion as to the time of death.

In cross-examination by Sir Edward Marshall Hall, Dr. Cadman said that when he gave as his opinion on the Friday night that the girl had been dead twenty-four hours he had no knowledge of the circumstances which led to the murder. He gave an entirely impartial and independent judgment. In further cross-examination he admitted that he had stated the time—twenty-four hours—at both the inquest and the police court proceedings. He still retained that opinion. Marshall Hall then replied that he would not pursue the point, because if the witness thought that twenty-four hours was the limit of time, then eleven o'clock on the Thursday night was the earliest hour at which Irene Munro could have been killed. Dr. Cadman answered: "Decidedly."

Re-examined by Mr. Gill, the doctor at first denied that in his examination-in-chief he said that the condition in which he first saw the body was consistent with death having occurred on Thursday afternoon, but he did not wish to withdraw the statement because it was the case. He based his opinion upon blood flowing from the left nostril when the body was moved. If death had taken place earlier than twenty-four hours, he would have expected the blood to be coagulated. There was no re-cross-examination by either defending counsel.

Dr. Adams gave evidence of the results of the post-mortem examination he made on the body of Irene Munro.

He first saw it at 2.30 on Saturday, August 21. After describing the manifold injuries to the face and head, which could have been caused by the brick, witness stated that the first severe blow on the left side of the head produced unconsciousness, and death resulted from injury to the brain. In cross-examination by Marshall Hall the witness gave as his opinion that one or more blows had been struck before the brick was used. The penetrating wound in the front of the face which knocked out two teeth and dislodged two others, was probably, but not necessarily, caused by a sharp instrument, "something like a stick with a point." The question of *rigor mortis* was then thoroughly investigated, the witness giving it as his opinion that what Dr. Cadman took for blood flowing from the nostril had been a very fine serum, or discharge, resembling blood. The witness was not asked at the inquest or the police court proceedings to express any view as to the time limit.

The examination and cross-examination of Dr. Elworthy, who made a further post-mortem examination of the body of Irene Munro on August 25 in the presence of Dr. Adams, supported the previous witness's evidence as to the nature and cause of the injuries and the weapons utilized. Dr. Elworthy was of opinion that if an examination had been made, either by Dr. Cadman when he first saw the body, or at the earlier post-mortem on August 21, to discover the temperature of the inside of the body it would have thrown more light on the time when death occurred. A re-examination by Mr. Gill elicited the opinion from the witness that when Dr. Cadman first saw the body the conditions were quite consistent with death having taken place between 3.30 and 5.30 in the afternoon.

Evidence was given by John Webster, official analyst to the Home Office, of having examined the stone found near the body. He discovered certain stains which, on being analysed, were human blood.

Dorothy Ducker gave evidence relating to the visits of Field and Gray to the Albemarle on August 19. She remem-

bered them first coming in just after twelve o'clock, and the
episode of Gray's asking for biscuits for his dog. Shown a
stick in Court, the witness considered it "something like"
the one Gray had held up, but would not swear that it was
the same, as she had not had a good look at the original.
She remembered the dog's head. In cross-examination by
Mr. Cassels the witness stated that she had not seen the
stick before the 19th, and never in the possession of Field.
Cross-examined by Marshall Hall, Miss Ducker remained
positive that the date of the stick episode was the 19th,
and not, as suggested to her by defending counsel, a week
earlier. She did not mention a stick when giving evidence
before the coroner on September 21 as she had no recol-
lection then of the incident, but when the murder was being
discussed in the hotel bar on a later date a customer
remarked that the crime might have been committed with
a stick. This brought back to the witness's mind the stick
she had seen in Gray's hand, and she replied that she
remembered it. Afterwards she made a statement to this
effect to the authorities. Elsie Finley, Miss Ducker's fellow-
barmaid, corroborated certain of her colleague's evidence as
to the drinks offered to both by Gray on the evening of the
19th, and the expensive cigarettes which the two men were
smoking. In cross-examination this young lady proved more
than a match for Marshall Hall. She fell into none of his
obvious traps, and "did not remember" a good many
incidents about which he questioned her.

The evidence of Blackmer, Rogers, Verrall, Dyer, and
Jupp followed. Blackmer positively identified Field and
Gray as alighting from the omnibus at the Archery, and immediately afterwards being accosted by a girl. This was
obviously when Irene Munro had just come out of 393 Seaside, and immediately before she went back there for her
coat. Rogers and Verrall knew her by sight as a lodger in
the house where both were working, and were agreed as
to seeing her leave it shortly before three o'clock on the
Thursday afternoon and go towards the Archery. Verrall

gave evidence of seeing her walking past almost immediately afterwards, accompanied by two men. Dyer recognized Gray a little later, with another man and a girl, his statement that he pointed out Gray to his fellow-workmate Jupp, speaking of him by name, being corroborated in the latter's evidence. Next followed that of Putland and Wells.

The story of these two pointed overwhelmingly to the accused as Irene Munro's companions. Putland had seen her twice before, alone on the Tuesday, and with the same men on the Wednesday. Both he and Wells picked out Field as one of the men they had followed on the Thursday and recognized on the Friday with two different girls. Both the defending counsel endeavoured somewhat unchivalrously to discredit the value of these witnesses' evidence by insinuating in cross-examination that they had gone after the trio to the Crumbles for purposes of blackmail, but the Judge objected, pointing out that evidence had been called which gave Putland and Wells good characters by previous employers, and that curiosity, possibly not of a wholly admirable kind, had been their sole motive in acting as they did.

The next witnesses were Mrs. Wynniatt, whose evidence shed no light on Irene Munro's death, and the five railwaymen. Their evidence was very similar, emphasizing the high spirits of the girl and her companions, but their descriptions of the latter were vague, and they all admitted to having been unable to pick out either of the accused at the identity parade. Evidence was then given as to the visit of Field and Gray to the Hippodrome on the night of the 19th, the amount spent on drinks, and the borrowed money Field paid back. Hilda Maud Baxter then related her first meeting with the prisoners at the pillar-box in St. John's Road the same evening. She stated that she had been in service in Eastbourne since July 29, but had never spoken to Field and Gray before the 19th. She could not remember which of them asked if they might walk home with her. No names were mentioned, and she did not know who they were. She denied that there was a word of truth in their story that she had been with them at Pevensey on the Thursday afternoon and had ice-cream together. Elsie May Hawes and her sister-in-law, Jessie Hawes, stated that the previous August they were fellow-servants of Hilda Maud Baxter at Ravenhurst. On the 19th both witnesses had tea with her there, and she was not out during the afternoon.

Mrs. Munro's evidence was very brief. She stated that her daughter had never stayed out late at night, was particular about her associates, not fond of jewellery, and possessed none of any value. She always behaved well, and was neat and tidy. She discussed her work with her mother, but never brought her business friends home.

Archibald Thomas Darrington, the next witness, proved extremely damaging to the defence. He stated that when in Maidstone Prison on remand, charged with stealing a bicycle from outside the public library at Eastbourne, Gray spoke to him during exercise. He inquired where witness had been on the afternoon of August 19, and whether he was at the circus. Gray then asked if Darrington would say that he had been at the circus with him, but, without directly refusing, Darrington answered that he was in trouble enough himself. On another occasion Gray made further suggestions to the witness regarding a possible alibi for the 19th, before they were cautioned by a warder for talking and separated. The evidence of two warders from the prison corroborated Darrington's story that there had been more than one illicit conversation during exercise between him and Gray.

A convict named William Smith stated that during the previous September he was at Maidstone Prison, serving a six months' sentence for theft. He admitted that he had several previous convictions. During his term of imprisonment he did not receive any letters and had no access to newspapers. Part of his work consisted of cleaning the landing outside his cell. Gray was in a cell along the same landing. Smith did not know why he was there, but Gray spoke to him through the grating across the cell doorway, and told him that he was "in for murder." Smith remarked that Gray was unlucky, and Gray went on to say: "But they cannot prove it. Though I was with the girl almost to the hour she died, that does not mean to say I done it." Various other conversations took place between Smith and Gray, Gray telling Smith that he was going to persuade another man (presumably Darrington) to say that he saw a sailor with the girl. He also gave Smith certain messages for "his mate" (Field), which Smith stated he did not deliver. On September 25 a warder suspected that Smith and Gray were communicating with one another, a practice strictly forbidden by the prison regulations, and it was stopped. Smith knew no particulars of the Crumbles murder, but stated that he asked Gray how it was done, and Gray answered: "By dropping a heavy stone on her." Smith inquired how Gray knew this, and Gray replied that he had seen the stone and it was "a tidy-sized one." Eventually Smith made a statement to a warder, and later to the Prison Governor. He was emphatic that he received no bribe such as a remission of sentence for doing this, and knew that, on the contrary, he might have found himself involved in serious trouble for his breach of the prison rules.

The only witness for the defence was the accused Field. He stated that he was out of work since his discharge from the Navy, with the exception of four weeks' employment with the Eastbourne Electric Light Company, and in receipt of 29s. weekly from the Labour Exchange. He met Gray, who was likewise out of work, in June, 1920. His counsel then took Field through details of his movements on August 17, 18 and 19. Field now recollected the two early visits paid by himself and Gray to the Albemarle, and stated that he thought Gray was wearing a blue serge suit and a trilby hat. As Miss Ducker refused Gray's invitation to the pictures, he and witness decided to go for a walk.

Field now admitted that they took a bus from Leaf Hall to the Archery, and on alighting spoke to Blackmer, but averred that after Blackmer left them he and Gray went straight down Seaside towards Pevensey Bay. He denied that they met a girl at the Archery, or that any girl addressed him, saying "Hullo, Jack!" or was in the company of himself and Gray along the road. They did not go on to the Crumbles, but walked to Pevensey Castle, stayed there about ten minutes, and returned to Eastbourne by bus from the Lodge Inn. They went to Gray's house, where witness remained till six o'clock. By arrangement he called for Gray again after he had had tea at his own home. Gray had "smartened himself up a bit" by brushing his clothes and washing himself, but "he did not look exactly respectable." Witness denied that Gray had changed his suit.

Shown a stick, Field admitted that it belonged to his father, but denied that he had had it out with him on any occasion on the 19th. He had ceased to carry it for a fortnight or three weeks previously. The conversation about a stick and biscuits for a dog took place as far back as three weeks before the 19th. He acknowledged that he and Gray had attempted to enlist on Saturday (21st). He gave as reasons that Gray's pension had been reduced, and he (witness) knew that his unemployment benefit would not continue indefinitely. He alleged that he had instituted inquiries about enlisting before the 21st. He and Gray first made Miss Baxter's acquaintance on Sunday evening (22nd). When they had been detained by the police and were waiting for Chief Inspector Mercer to interview them, Field alleged that a certain conversation took place between himself and Gray, which the constable in charge had not overheard. They agreed to say that Miss Baxter had been with them at Pevensey on the Thursday afternoon. Asked why they had picked out the afternoon, Field replied: "Because we saw in the paper that the murder was supposed to have been committed after lunch-time, and that Miss Munro

was seen about three o'clock, or a girl like Miss
Munro, and therefore we knew it would have to be after
three, and we knew we could prove where we were
after six, and therefore we knew it would be between
three and six that we should want to prove where we
were."

In cross-examination Field again admitted the meeting
with Blackmer, but once more denied the accosting of him
(witness) by any girl at the Archery. He acknowledged that
if Dyer saw and recognized Gray he must have been Gray's
companion, but stated that the story of Putland and Wells
was entirely false. He persisted in denying that Gray had
changed his clothes that evening, although reminded that
Gray himself had admitted at the inquest that he did so,
and witness had heard him. Field denied a good deal of
Miss Baxter's story, and put up a good fight when con-
fronted with certain discrepancies between his statement
and Gray's, alleging that he had "forgotten" certain incidents. The only truth Field really uttered when in the
witness-box was the alleged words put into his mouth
afterwards by Gray: i.e., that he was telling lies from the
moment he entered it till he left it.

Gray did not take advantage of his privilege of giving
evidence on his own behalf. It would have been interesting
to hear what explanation, other than a blunt and unsub-
stantiated denial, he had to offer to refute the statements
of Darrington and Smith.

XI

On behalf of the prosecution Mr. Gill summed up the
evidence briefly. Dealing with the defence's suggestion that
the murder had been committed on the night of Thursday,
counsel contended that proof of the deceased girl being
seen walking towards the Crumbles with the two men at
2.30 in the afternoon was overwhelming. Unless she was
murdered during the afternoon, she would have returned

to her lodgings. The episode of the stick was highly significant. One answering the description had been found at Field's home, and the witness who described it as in the possession of one of the two men walking with a girl knew nothing of its production earlier in the same day at the Albemarle. Counsel then described the scene which he suggested occurred at the Crumbles. Whether the girl's money or her virtue was threatened, violence resulted, and when she had been stunned, the large stone produced in the case completed fatal injuries. Gray said the girl was killed by dropping a stone on her. "The prosecution is right," said Mr. Gill. "He knows."

Addressing the jury on behalf of Field, Mr. Cassels maintained that the case against him rested purely on circumstantial evidence. The men at the railway-hut had not identified either of the men. Blackmer dressed Irene Munro in blue, Putland in a green coat with black accessories, and Wells in a hat which was not the one with her when her body was found. A pointed correction by the Judge was hurriedly answered, and counsel went on to allude to Wells's statement that Irene Munro was wearing a checked skirt and a black blouse. Were the jury to accept impressions of witnesses in such a matter? It was difficult to conceive that the crime had been committed in broad daylight, in view of the railway-hut and the windows of adjacent cottages. If the jury accepted Dr. Cadman's evidence as to the time of death, there was an end to the case for the prosecution. There was no evidence to support the Crown's theory that the girl was killed in resisting an assault. The theory that the same evening the two men were spending money stolen from Irene Munro's bag was unsupported, as their expenditure did not total 25s. There was no evidence that the accused endeavoured to persuade Miss Baxter to support them in a false alibi. They had not altered their mode of living after the 19th. Nobody saw them coming back from the Crumbles, and if they were seen going there they could have been seen returning. Mr. Cassels finally suggested that the murder took place later in the day than the prosecution had alleged.

Sir Edward Marshall Hall, speaking on Gray's behalf, contended that Irene Munro had been a pleasure-loving girl, fond of expensive entertainments, but ladylike, educated, and fastidious as to her choice of company. It was incredible that she should have made the acquaintance of two "down-and-outs" like the prisoners, and gone about with them. Turning to the medical evidence, counsel submitted that Dr. Cadman's opinion as to the time of death deserved careful consideration. If the murder had taken place in the afternoon, the girl's scream of fear and apprehension as she was struck in the face must have been audible for a great distance, as well as the noise made by shovelling the shingle over the body. Surely the crime was committed under cover of darkness, as corroborated by Dr. Cadman's view as to the time of death? Dealing with motive, Gray's remark that they would have more money in the evening might seem to infer that he and Field had arranged to rob and murder the girl they had met the previous day, but Irene Munro was not worth robbing. There was no evidence of assault, and none of concerted action or premeditation. The discrepancies between the evidence of witnesses as to the colour of the men's suits were stressed by counsel. He also said that as Field had appeared in the witness-box there was no necessity for Gray to give evidence. If Field were not believed by the jury, neither would Gray have been. If the jury could not accept the evidence put forward by the prosecution as conclusive, the accused were entitled to a verdict of "Not guilty."

XII

Mr. Justice Avory began his summing up with the usual warning to the jury that they were to pay no attention to what they had heard or read in connexion with the case

prior to the trial, but were to arrive at a verdict based solely
on the evidence given in Court. With admirable, and possibly quite unconscious, alliteration, the Judge added: "I
regret that such a warning in a Criminal Court of this
country should be rendered necessary by the pernicious
practice which prevails of pandering to the prurient pro-
clivities of the public by publishing, pictorially or otherwise,
the lurid details of a ghastly tragedy such as that which we
are investigating."

Continuing, his Lordship said that both men were jointly
charged with the wilful murder of Irene Munro on
August 19 last. The joint charge meant that they were acting together, one aiding and abetting the other, and it was
immaterial which man actually committed the violence that
killed her. There could be no doubt that the girl was murdered, and that whoever murdered her took possession of
her handbag, containing her money and keys, and threw
the latter away. Could the jury have any doubt that if one
of the accused was guilty both were? It had been admitted
that they were in each other's company all that afternoon
and evening. Where one went, the other went; each must
have known what his companion did; and after the evidence
given the jury must say whether they could doubt if guilt
had been brought home to one, it had not been equally
brought home to both.

Dealing with the question of motive, the Judge said that,
subject to the jury's better judgment, it seemed to him to be
immaterial. Whoever murdered the girl did it from some
motive, either robbery, under a misapprehension that she
was in possession of more money than turned out to be the
case, or to combat her resistance to an attempted assault,
as possibly evidenced by the scratches found inside her
right thigh. It was unnecessary for the jury to decide how
she was murdered, whether with a blow from a stick or a
fist, the injuries being completed by the brick, the only way
in which the stick became material being Field's denial that
he had had any stick in his possession that afternoon. If

they came to the conclusion that he had with him the stick
produced in Court, or another, as he walked towards the
Crumbles, they must consider what inference was to be
drawn from his denying this fact. It was not disputed that
the prisoners, or certainly Field, were spending money
freely later in the evening. The jury were advised not to
pay too much attention to this as it was not disputed that
Field had drawn 29s. in unemployment pay that morning.
The prosecution had suggested that if the prisoners had
killed the girl and stolen her bag then they would have been
in possession of money that evening, but the amount expended by them was not more than Field had had earlier
in the day without the contents of Irene Munro's purse.
For that reason it seemed to his Lordship to be a small
matter.

After explaining fully the meaning of the term "circumstantial evidence," the Judge turned to the time factor in
the case. The result of the medical evidence, into which
his Lordship did not propose to go in detail, was that
everything was consistent with death having taken place in
the afternoon of the 19th. The jury should ask themselves
the question why the prisoners on the 24th, the Tuesday
following the murder, arranged between themselves to set
up a false alibi for the afternoon of the 19th, unless they
knew that the murder had been committed then. Sir Edward
Marshall Hall, in his speech on behalf of Gray, had drawn
the jury's attention to certain statements in a newspaper
published the previous day, and alleged that these explained
why the prisoners feared arrest. It was significant, the Judge
went on, if they had obtained the information which alarmed
them from this same newspaper, that in more than one
place it suggested that the crime took place at night.
How did it come about that, as Field had told them,
they prepared a false alibi for the afternoon unless
they knew that the crime was committed in the afternoon?

After dealing with the general outline of the case as

presented by the prosecution, the Judge reminded the jury of Gray's change of clothes, and the attempt of Field and himself to enlist directly news of the finding of the body was made public. They need not necessarily have given their own names and addresses, the Judge pointed out, as a great many men would never have been accepted in the Army had they not furnished false particulars about themselves. Referring to the defence's suggestion that it was incredible that men who had just committed such a crime could calmly embark on an acquaintance with another girl the same evening and arrange to meet her again, and to continue their ordinary mode of living for days afterwards, the Judge asked the jury to reflect whether a man or men capable of committing an act such as this one would not be capable of anything.

In dealing directly with the evidence, the Judge touched upon the main outlines of Miss Ducker's story. He stressed the fact that Field admitted that he sometimes carried a stick similar to the one produced in Court, but that it was the property of his father. This was of importance, as if it had any connexion with the murder the natural thing would have been for him to attempt to get rid of it. Suspicion might have been aroused when his father inquired for it, which was probably why he did not throw it away. The statements of Blackmer, Verrall, Dyer, and Jupp could be relied upon to prove that at about three o'clock the two prisoners were seen walking towards the Crumbles with a girl, and the jury had to consider was she the deceased one? If she were not, why did they—or one of them—now swear that they were never in the company of any girl at all that afternoon?

Alluding to the descriptions given by the different witnesses of what the girl they saw was wearing, the Judge suggested that men of their type would not necessarily be good judges of a woman's clothes. The dress which Blackmer called a blue one was not inconsistent with its being the grey coat-frock produced in Court. Verrall had said that the men he saw with Irene Munro both wore grey suits. Evidence had been called to show that Gray undoubtedly had a light grey suit, and Field's suit might have been called a dark or grey coat and trousers.

The evidence of Putland and Wells was fully dealt with, the Judge warmly repudiating defending counsel's earlier suggestion that Putland was a discreditable witness because he might have had blackmail in his mind as a motive for following the people he saw. The evidence of the five railwaymen was next gone into briefly as establishing the identity of the men they saw with Irene Munro. The Judge then described Field and Gray as men of plausible manners and address, possessed of enough money for amusement, and in the habit of entering into conversation with girls along the Parade at Eastbourne. Irene Munro was a typist on holiday, in a humble position of life, and although the picture of her drawn by the defence as a particular girl regarding her associates, and quiet and refined, might be true, his Lordship thought it not unlikely that, alone in a strange place, she might, for the sake of companionship, have allowed these men to make her acquaintance. When in the witness-box Field had boasted of his politeness to everyone, and was quite capable of being agreeable to a solitary young girl. Could the jury feel any doubt, having regard to all the evidence, that she was in the prisoners' company on the 19th and on the previous day as well?

Finally, the Judge dealt minutely with Field's statement and his evidence on his own behalf. Miss Baxter's story contradicted Field's. Why should both men have anticipated arrest merely because they wore grey suits? Why did Field persist in saying that Gray had not changed his clothes on the evening of the 19th, although Gray admitted at the inquest that he did so, when Miss Ducker stated the same? With regard to Gray's statement, there need not necessarily have been any great amount of blood upon the person of whoever committed the crime, but there might

have been some, and a person scraping the shingle would
very likely get his suit soiled. That might be a sufficient
reason for Gray changing his clothes, but why did Field
persist on oath that Gray had not done so? Referring to
the evidence of Darrington and Smith, the Judge stressed
its significance, and reminded the jury that because these
were not men of good character it did not necessarily mean
that their word must be unworthy of credence.

XIII

The jury retired at four minutes past two and returned into
Court at seven minutes past three. In answer to the question of the Clerk of the Court, their foreman said that they
were agreed upon their verdict. They found both prisoners
guilty, but—an inexplicable and amazing sidelight upon the
mentality of a British jury—they asked that the men might
be recommended to mercy on the ground that the jury were
of opinion that the crime was not premeditated. Neither
man had anything to say in mitigation of sentence, and
Mr. Justice Avory immediately dealt faithfully with both.
They stood convicted of a foul and brutal murder. The
defence which they had concocted had been shown to be
untrue. They must prepare themselves to undergo the
penalty exacted by the law. The recommendation to mercy
would be forwarded to the proper quarter and would
receive due consideration. Formal sentence of death was
then passed in each case, the Judge directing that it should
be carried out at Wandsworth Prison.

Field and Gray were at once taken below. In order to
substantiate or deny Gray's subsequent story as to what,
he alleged, took place shortly between himself and Field,
it is necessary to follow very carefully the incidents of their
removal to Wandsworth, as testified to by other witnesses.
Both men remained in two separate cells, each under the
charge of warders. When the time came for their removal,
Gray, with his guards, was taken in a cab to Lewes railway

station, and Field, similarly escorted, followed in another cab. There was no opportunity for any conversation between the two men. The warders had received orders to keep them apart, and did so. Gray and his companions arrived first at the station; Field, with his, a few seconds later. The whole party went direct to the station-master's office, there to await the London train. Field and Gray sat on two chairs, with another piece of furniture between them, and one of the warders in charge of Field sat close beside him. The only remark made by Gray that the warder overheard was a request for a cigarette. This was allowed to both men, and Field then said to Gray: "Isn't it a treat to get a cigarette?" and Gray agreed. The alleged conversation between Field and Gray took place, the latter averred, "in bits," but the warders in charge, who never left the prisoners the whole time, heard nothing of it.

On December 29 Gray informed the Deputy Governor of Wandsworth that he wished to make a statement. As Gray could not read or write, this was written down for him at his dictation by the Deputy Governor and after Gray had signed it (presumably by affixing his mark), the Deputy Governor and the Chief Warder both witnessed it. On January 4 Field said that he also wished to make a statement, and was allowed to do so. Three days later Field's statement was given to Gray, and read over to him by the Deputy Governor, as well as statements made by the warders who had accompanied the two men from the Assize Court to Wandsworth. Gray seemed to understand the purport of all these documents, but made no comment. Field was likewise shown a copy of Gray's statement. On January 13 both men sent in a petition to the Home Secretary, intimating that they wished to appeal against their convictions and sentences.

XIV

The appeals were heard jointly by the Court of Criminal

Appeal on Monday and Tuesday, January 17 and 18, before the Lord Chief Justice (Lord Reading), Mr. Justice Bray, and Mr. Justice Acton. Mr. Cassels appeared for Field, Sir Edward Marshall Hall, K.C., and Mr. Flowers for Gray, and Sir Charles Gill, K.C., and Mr. Whiteley for the Crown. Mr. Cassels said that the case of Field came before the Court (1) on appeal by the man himself; (2) on an application by counsel on the appellant's behalf to call further evidence; and (3) on reference by the Home Secretary upon a petition presented by the appellant for mercy. Sir Edward Marshall Hall also made application that Gray should be allowed to appear in the witness-box. Sir Charles Gill said the Crown was prepared to deal with the evidence, if it were given, and he raised no objection. The Lord Chief Justice stated that before they came to any decision as to the other witnesses they would hear the evidence of the appellants themselves.

Field was heard first. Examined by his counsel, he stated that on Tuesday, August 17, he met Gray early in the forenoon, and they walked along the sea-front. On the way back they saw a girl evidently looking for something. Gray wished her "Good morning," but received no reply. Later, Gray boasted to Field that he would speak to and walk with her before the day was out. During the afternoon they met her near the Albemarle Hotel, and when Gray again accosted her she stopped and spoke to them. He asked her where she was going, and she answered: "For a walk." The three went together to Beachy Head, remaining there till it was nearly dark. They parted at Eastbourne railway station, where the girl caught a bus, after having arranged to meet them again next day at the Archery Tavern. On Wednesday, August 18, Field and Gray met in the morning and spent it on the sea-front. After lunch they rejoined each other at the Albemarle and went by bus to the Archery where they met the girl. The trio walked to Pevensey Bay. Field alleged that on the way the girl seemed to resent his being there, and would have preferred the company of

Gray. He tried to be pleasant to her and considered that he succeeded just as they were returning. Gray and he left her about six o'clock, after arranging to meet again as before at the Archery the following afternoon.

Field stated that on the Thursday morning (August 19) he went first to the Labour Exchange and drew his unemployment benefit of 29s. He then met Gray, and after having coffee, for which Field paid on the Parade, they went to the Albemarle at midday. They remained till 1.15, Field paying for the refreshment they had. Outside they parted, Gray returning home for dinner, and Field going to a restaurant for his. Afterwards Field called for Gray at his house, and they boarded a bus going to the Archery. Field noticed an official on it who was wearing a new uniform and when they alighted he drew the man's attention to this. Just then the girl crossed the road and called out to witness: "Hullo, Jack!" The three walked to the Crumbles and went on to the railway-line. Field stated that he was on the girl's left-hand side and at the time did not know her name. They passed the railway-hut. He picked up a stray kitten which the girl stroked. Field alleged that it was he who put the kitten in at the door of the hut, not Gray, who was walking in front of him with the girl, either arm-in-arm, or with his arm round her waist. After passing the hut, Gray hinted that he should prefer Field to leave them, and Field asked the girl whether she would object if he did, as he wanted a good walk. The girl replied that she did not mind, and he left her and Gray alone and walked on to the gates of Pevensey Castle. He came back by the road, and towards Pevensey Bay he met Gray by himself. Field asked him where the girl was, and Gray alleged that they had quarrelled and she had gone home. He and Field walked to the Lodge Inn where they boarded an Eastbourne bus. Gray paid the fares, which puzzled Field, as he himself had done so previously, and stood drinks. Questioned, Gray said that he had had the money all the time.

Afterwards Field returned home, and later in the evening

he and Gray went to the Albemarle. Here Gray paid for
drinks for the two barmaids. When Field asked him where
he had obtained the money, Gray replied: "Shut up and
mind your own business! I'm paying for the drinks and
that is all that concerns you." The two went to the Hippodrome, left it for another visit to the Albemarle, and then
returned to the Hippodrome. They did not meet Miss
Baxter that night. Gray was in Field's company the whole
time until they parted outside the Hippodrome at 10.50.
Field reached his house at eleven o'clock and did not go
out again that night. He and his brother slept together.
His family were at home, his mother having just returned
from London.

On Friday Field was about with Gray. They visited the
Albemarle and a couple of picture-houses. On Saturday
Field left his home about 9 a.m. and saw on the placards
that a dead body had been found on the Crumbles. He
bought a paper and took it round to Gray's house. As Gray
could not read, Field read the account aloud to him. Gray
became excited and said that he had been with the girl on
Thursday evening, that she said something he did not like
and he had kicked her. She was lying on the beach at the
time, and frightened, he covered her over with shingle.
Had Field not left them, it would not have happened. He
begged Field to say nothing for the sake of his (Gray's)
wife, adding that it might "blow over." Field promised
to do his best and if Gray were arrested agreed to say that
they had been at Pevensey together. The suggestion of their
enlisting came from Gray. Field further alleged that Gray
promised to stand by him and if Field were involved in the
matter he would clear him by telling the truth. They spent
Saturday afternoon and evening together, and were in each
other's company all Sunday. Gray seemed agitated and
imagined that people were staring at him. In the afternoon
they met Miss Baxter and discussed the murder. Gray told
her that he and Field might be arrested as they both had
grey suits, and Miss Baxter said that in that event she would

tell the police that they were with her at Pevensey on the 19th. Field told Gray that this would be found sooner or later to be untrue, but Gray insisted that if arrested he would say that he had been with Miss Baxter all the afternoon.

Field further stated that Gray's statement that he was with him (witness) at Pevensey on August 19 was not true. His evidence at the trial was also false. He and Gray had no conversation whilst waiting in the station-master's office at Lewes station, after their conviction and sentence. Field maintained that he had stood by Gray to the end, but when he made his statement on January 4 he thought for the sake of his parents that he ought to say what actually happened. What he put in this statement was true.

Cross-examined by Sir Edward Marshall Hall, Field said that the statement was in his handwriting, and no one had prompted the contents. Gray did not tell him that he had killed Irene Munro. He said that he had hit her and covered her with beach. Field did not understand whether she had died from Gray's attack upon her or been smothered by the shingle. He put great faith in Gray's promise that if he (Field) were involved in the crime Gray would confess the truth. Asked why he did not mention this promise in his statement of January 4, Field replied that "he did not think about it." He now admitted that practically the whole of the evidence called by the prosecution regarding his identity was true.

Cross-examined by Sir Charles Gill, Field alleged that on the afternoon of the 19th Gray was wearing a blue serge suit, and in the evening a grey one. He heard four witnesses who saw the three pass the hut say that the shorter man of the two was walking linked with the girl, but alleged that he had never worn a blue serge suit in his life, and that it was he, not Gray, who put the kitten in at the hut door. He denied that he struck the girl when she resented his attempting to take liberties with her. Asked why they had taken Irene Munro to the Crumbles, Field answered that

she wanted a walk, and herself suggested going there. Gray
told witness that he had struck her almost immediately after
Field had left them. He understood that Gray had buried
her alive. When he went off, he told Gray that he was going
to Pevensey. He did not hear Gray say in the Albemarle
that they would have more money that night. Gray apparently had none when he went on the Crumbles, but had
some when he came off. Field concluded that he had robbed
the girl whom he attacked and buried. Field stood by him
afterwards because they were friends and for the sake of
Gray's wife. When they attempted to enlist, Field knew
that he would not be accepted. Pressed by the Lord Chief
Justice for the reason, Field said that he had been discharged from the Navy, and the cause for this was stated
on his papers.

In continued cross-examination by Sir Charles Gill, Field
admitted that on Saturday morning he and Gray arranged
their false alibi for Thursday afternoon. His early statement that he and Gray were with Miss Baxter then was
untrue. When a verdict of "Wilful murder" was returned
against both at the inquest, Field did not call upon Gray to
clear him because "I was told by my solicitor that the
Coroner's inquest did not matter." When the verdict was
given at the trial, Field relied upon the recommendation
to mercy and "was not going to give Gray away then."
Asked why when he sent in his appeal, which disclosed no
grounds in substance, he had not made a true statement,
Field replied: "I thought the appeal would go through and
we should get off." In answer to the Lord Chief Justice,
Field admitted that, although Gray acknowledged that he
had struck the girl into unconsciousness and buried her
possibly alive, he himself continued on intimate terms with
Gray. Gray's wife had asked him (Field) to associate with
her husband as he had no other men friends. Field was
willing, if both men were reprieved, to go to penal servitude
in order that Gray might ultimately rejoin his wife. Field
was not related to her in any way.

Gray gave evidence next. Examined by Sir Edward Marshall Hall, he stated that on the morning of August 19 he met Field at ten o'clock and remained with him till 12.30. They visited the Albemarle together. Gray had a midday meal at his own house, and Field called for him there at two o'clock. They returned to the Albemarle, remaining for half an hour. Field then suggested that he and Gray should go to Pevensey Castle. Gray alleged that he refused as he had no money and did not like to be indebted to Field for the bus fares. He left Field at 2.30 and returned home, reaching it at 2.45. He did not see Field again until 6.40, when Field called at his house. They visited the Hippodrome together and were in each other's company till 10.30. It was untrue that he confessed to Field that he had struck and buried Irene Munro. He was not with her at all on Thursday afternoon. He knew nothing about the girl's death. After being sentenced, he was taken to the cells and then to Lewes railway station. Gray then repeated the story contained in his statement of December 29 which was, briefly, that whilst waiting for the train between 4.45 and 6.11 Field confessed to him that after he and Gray parted at 10.30 on the night of August 19 Irene Munro came up and asked him her way. According to Gray, Field admitted that he and the girl walked some distance together in conversation, that something he said displeased her, and she slapped his face. He saw nobody about and struck her. He left her lying unconscious, and walked away, but fearing that she might recover and report him to the police, he returned and "gave her another hit," which "put her right out." Gray alleged that Field promised to tell the Prison Governor that he was innocent, and if this did not free Gray, Field would communicate with *John Bull* and say that Gray had had nothing to do with the murder. In his notice of appeal Gray had made no mention of this conversation, but on December 29 his statement was written down for him.

Cross-examined by Mr. Cassels, Gray stated that before

this alleged confession on December 17 Field had never promised to say anything to exculpate himself. Asked why he did not say that he was at his home on the afternoon of the 19th, Gray replied at first: "Because Field said that we were at Pevensey," but, on being pressed, alleged that he had "kept quiet" on account of having committed a theft during the material time about which the police knew. He had been at the Eastbourne swimming-baths by himself on the 19th, remaining from 3.15 till four. Whilst there he stole a wallet containing money from another bather's box. Reminded by Mr. Cassels that this robbery had taken place on the 14th, Gray replied that this was a second theft, committed on the 19th. He was the thief on both occasions, and had been alone each time.

Further cross-examined, Gray denied that he was at the Archery with Field on the Thursday afternoon. He had never walked with Field towards the Crumbles. All the witnesses were wrong who said that they saw him doing so. He was wearing a navy blue suit and a brown round cap. He paid for the drinks on the night of the 19th with the money stolen from the swimming-baths. According to the way Field spoke to him, the murder was committed at night. Cross-examined by Sir Charles Gill, Gray maintained that he was at the swimming-baths from 3.15 till four, after which he went home.

Four warders—Robert William O'Callaghan, Henry Jackson, Arthur Sargant, and Samuel Percy Johnson—gave evidence of events in the station-master's office after the Assize trial. All were agreed that there was no conversation between the condemned men. Gray asked for a cigarette, and he and Field were allowed to smoke by permission of the Prison Governor.

Herbert Field, examined by Mr. Cassels, stated that the previous August he was living at 23 Susans Road, Eastbourne. On the night of the 19th he slept at home. He came in about eleven o'clock and found his brother Jack having supper. His brother did not go out again that night, or get up during it. They went to bed between 11.30 and 11.45.

Mrs. Field, mother of the last witness, corroborated his statement. Examined by Mr. Cassels, she said that on August 19 about seven in the evening she returned from a five days' visit to London. Her son Jack was then out, but came home shortly before eleven o'clock. Both her sons slept in the kitchen. She left them there at 11.30 and heard nobody leave the house during the night.

James Woolgar, an attendant at the Devonshire Park Swimming-baths at Eastbourne, examined by Sir Charles Gill, stated that he knew both prisoners. They had been together at the baths on the morning of August 14. Between 12.30 and 12.45 a bather named Saunders complained that his wallet had been stolen, and the police were communicated with. The witness was suspicious of Field and Gray, as he knew that both were out of work, and when they came to the baths on the 17th at 10.30 a.m. Woolgar informed the police and the two men were kept under observation. This was the last time they visited the baths. Gray was not there on the afternoon of the 19th, nor was any theft reported on that date.

Mr. Cassels's address on behalf of Field ended the first day's proceedings. At the second and concluding day's hearing of the appeals Sir Edward Marshall Hall spoke on behalf of Gray. The Lord Chief Justice then delivered the judgment of the Court. In the unanimous opinion of the three judges who heard the fresh evidence, each man had merely concocted an improbable story throwing the responsibility for the crime on the other, and their stories had been amply disproved by the statements of additional witnesses. Both appeals were unhesitatingly dismissed.

XV

On Friday, February 4, 1921, the last grim scene in the Crumbles tragedy of nearly six months previously was enacted at Wandsworth. Between the appeals and the double execution Field and Gray had been kept in separate cells and only saw each other again just as they approached the scaffold. Neither made any confession, but a curious light is shown on the mentality of certain people who take an interest in sensational crimes by a message left by both men to the effect that they wished to express their gratitude for letters and expressions of sympathy sent to them whilst awaiting execution. It is a little difficult to see what sympathy was required or deserved by the two brutal slayers of a defenceless girl of seventeen however misguided she may have been, but as the Lancashire proverb has it: "There's nowt so queer as folk."

Irene Munro's story might well be called "A Warning to Frolics." The girl's incredible folly at first detracts from any sympathy felt for her. In defence of it one can only plead her youth, her early years overshadowed by the war, the emancipation which women were just then beginning to experience and enjoy, her loneliness in a strange place, and her undoubted weakness for the opposite sex. Certain medical pronouncements proved that she must have been over-sexed and slightly abnormal. There is no evidence, beyond Field's before the Court of Criminal Appeal, to show how she actually came into contact with her two destroyers, but in all likelihood he spoke the truth for once when he said that Gray accosted her on the Tuesday afternoon and she responded. Of the ultimate guilt of both men there cannot be the faintest doubt, but how far murder, deliberate, calculated, cold-blooded, entered into their propositions when they first sought her company remains an enigma. If they surmised that she carried money in her handbag and purposed to rob her of it, why did they not do so when alone with her in the late evening on two occasions, first at Beachy Head and again at Pevensey? On the 19th they voluntarily drew Blackmer's attention to themselves a few seconds before she crossed the road to speak to them. If they had had any sinister motive in taking her to the Crumbles, why did they choose broad daylight of an August afternoon for their purpose? The girl's condition at the time precluded her having any immoral intention in her mind, supposing that she, a stranger to Eastbourne, knew of the reputation of the place to which she was going, and the fact that she went with two men exculpates her further. In all likelihood an attempt was made to snatch her handbag, and when she resisted or threatened police retaliation, one or other struck her with the stick carried by Field. Whose was the hand which lifted the iron-stone brick and dashed it down on her unconscious, unprotected face cannot be stated with certainty, but of the pair of callous scamps Gray emerges from the maze of evidence as the more brutal, and in all probability his rage overmastered prudence, common sense, consequences. The sea lapped in the distance; the sun beat down on the long expanse of beach, as two men with frantic haste shovelled the loose shingle over the green coat that clothed their still living victim before running from the spot. Chance plays a large part in the detection of murder. If they had stayed to bury her a little deeper that betraying foot would not have told of a dastardly crime, and Irene Munro might have lain in her shingly grave, none suspecting, until all danger to her slayers was past.

The murderer's victim seldom takes on any personality. He or she as a rule remains shadowy, vague, unreal, a peg on which to hang the story. Irene Munro, dead twenty-seven years, continues curiously vital and alive, a little ghost in a green coat, laughing as she walks to her doom. Fate took her to Eastbourne, and there Fate threw Field and Gray across her path. On that ill-omened Thursday afternoon it may well be asked, as it was of Hardy's doomed Tess, where was her guardian angel? "Perhaps, like that other god of whom the ironical Tishbite spoke, he was talking, or he was pursuing, or he was on a journey, or peradventure he was sleeping and not to be awaked." If she had again ignored Gray when he tried the second time to make her acquaintance, or if Putland and Wells had gone a little farther after the trio, the tragedy which overtook all of them might never have been. Irene Munro, the born murderee, in a sense brought her fate upon herself, and like Webster's ill-starred duchess, she died young.

GEORGE JOSEPH SMITH

(1915)

By Eric R. Watson

I

GEORGE JOSEPH SMITH, the most atrocious English criminal since Palmer, was born on January 11, 1872, at 92 Roman Road, Bethnal Green, his father being George Thomas Smith, an insurance agent, and his mother Louisa Smith, *née* Gibson. The son early displayed criminal tendencies, and seems to have been sent to the reformatory at Gravesend at the tender age of nine, remaining there till he was sixteen.

. When he left the reformatory he went to live with his mother, but he speedily took to evil courses, and got seven days for a small theft. That would be about the year 1890. On February 7, 1891, he was sentenced to six months' hard labour at Lambeth Police Court, in the name of George Smith, for stealing a bicycle. He stated to Miss Thornhill, his only lawful wife, that he served three years in the Northamptonshire Regiment, and he referred to a service with it to Sergeant Page on his arrest, while to the witness Crabbe he referred in vaguer terms to a period of military service when he was a gymnasium instructor. The police attach little importance to this supposed devotion to Mars. What is incontrovertible is that on July 24, 1896, he received twelve months' hard labour at the North London Sessions for larceny and receiving—three cases in all—in the name of George Baker. At this time he was known to the police as an associate of a woman unknown, whom he placed in various situations and induced to steal for him.

After coming out of prison, he proceeded to Leicester, where he opened a baker's shop at 28 Russell Square.

97

While residing there he met, towards the end of 1897, Caroline Beatrice Thornhill, and, after a short acquaintance, during which he suggested cohabitation without marriage, married her on January 17, 1898, at St. Matthew's Church, her relatives, who strongly disapproved of the bridegroom, not attending the ceremony. The bride had previously been a friend of a girl he employed in his shop, and she was only eighteen or nineteen years of age at the time. On this occasion Smith gave the name of George Oliver Love, and described his father as a detective of the name of George Love. The business failed in about six months. "Mrs. Love" went to a cousin in Nottingham, where "Mr. Love" pursued her.

Bringing "Mrs. Love" with him to London, he forced her to take various situations in London, for which he supplied the reference—posing as her late employer. He himself did no work. He also obtained situations for her at various places on the south coast, such as Brighton, Hove and Hastings. At the last-mentioned resort the unhappy "Mrs. Love" fell into the hands of the police. Without going into particulars, it suffices to say that Smith succeeded in making his escape for a while from the clutches of the law, only, however, to be arrested in London on November 11, 1900, on a charge preferred by his wife, whereupon he was taken to Hastings, and on January 9, 1901, two days before his twenty-ninth birthday, he was sentenced to two years' imprisonment, with hard labour, for receiving stolen goods. He remained in durance until October 10, 1902, when he was released, and he was next heard of in Leicester trying to find "Mrs. Love," but he did not succeed, her brothers chasing him out of the town. "Mrs. Love" had reason to fear for her safety if she remained anywhere within the reach of her George, and she accordingly left the country, taking ship to Canada, where she continued to dwell, except for a brief visit to Leicester in 1912 and 1913, until summoned back to England by Scotland Yard authorities in 1915.

Smith was not, however, without a second wife, even at this early stage. Partly for the gratification of his strong animal propensities, and even more because he much preferred to exploit women rather than work for himself or them, he had availed himself some time during 1899 of a temporary absence from his Beatrice to cast his basilisk glances over Miss ——, a very respectable and industrious boarding-house keeper in the metropolis. He went through a ceremony of marriage with her in 1899 at the register office, St. George's, Hanover Square. From time to time he would return to her, demanding money, and sometimes showing her large sums of gold, for the possession of which he would account as later he did to Miss Pegler. I shall recur to his relations with this unhappy woman in the concluding part of my narrative. Her last glimpse of Smith was through a grating looking out upon the exercise yard at Pentonville Prison, where her "husband," his sentence of death confirmed by the Court of Criminal Appeal, was in utter despondency pacing up and down, awaiting his removal to the gaol of Maidstone, the place appointed for him to expiate his iniquities.

Some time in 1908, in the name of George Love, he got some very subordinate employment in a West-End club; he seems to have been dismissed for inefficiency, so far as can be judged from a letter written when awaiting his trial for murder in Brixton Prison in 1915. This letter, characteristic for its vile grammar and spelling, its incoherence, and its braggart assumption of "my marked love of poetry and the fine arts," begged a favourable statement from the steward.

In June he was in Brighton, and he encountered on the front Mrs. F.W., a widow. He gave the name of George Joseph Smith, posed as a man of means, and pursued Mrs. W. to Worthing, where she was employed. The usual proposal of marriage followed; "he insisted on seeing my bank book." The amount was £33 13s. He professed to be a dealer in antiques; they remained at Worthing about three weeks, and the lady made arrangements to withdraw

her balance. She introduced him to Mrs. M——, a friend,
but the lady took an instant and violent dislike to the
antique dealer. On July 3 the happy pair went to Camden
Town Post Office to withdraw the money. Smith would
have appropriated the lot, but Mrs. W. left in £3 13s.; so
£20 in gold and two £5 notes were placed on the counter
and snatched up by Smith. "He knew I had no pocket,"
said Mrs. W.

The usual inexpensive jaunt followed—this time to the
White City—the usual excuse to leave the inamorata, the
usual speedy return to the apartments, and the usual lying
note about forwarding the box on. The total value of
Mrs. W.'s belongings that Smith took was about £80 to £90.

Now was about to begin the one romance of this sordid
life. Smith, with Mrs. W.'s money and effects, went to
Bristol, where he set up a small shop at 389 Gloucester
Road as a second-hand furniture dealer. At 368, in the
same road, dwelt Edith Mabel Pegler with her mother.
On July 1, 1908, she advertised for a situation as housekeeper, where a servant was kept. Smith replied to her
advertisement, and she speedily consented to keep house
for him, although he was not in a position to afford a
servant. After a week's acquaintance, Smith had so cap-
tivated Miss Pegler's maiden heart that she consented to
be his, although his means were very nebulous—a mythical
aunt who allowed him money, and "that he went about the
country dealing." The marriage was solemnized at St. Peter's
Register Office, Bristol, on July 30 by special licence, Smith
being married for the first time in his real name, describing
himself as thirty-three years of age, a bachelor and general
dealer, son of George Smith, deceased, figure artist.

Smith's relations to the only woman to whom he did not
behave with inhuman cruelty, although to her he lied and
to her begrudged the smallest sums of his ill-gotten wealth,
sufficiently appear from her evidence at the trial. Two
matters may here be noted, however. He gave poor Alice
Reavil's modest trousseau to his Edith, saying he had been

doing a deal in ladies' second-hand clothing. And it appeared from Miss Pegler's first statement to the police, taken by Detective-Inspector Cole and Sergeant Page in Bristol, that Smith only once during all the years she knew him had a bath, at Weston-super-Mare, and that he had never inquired at any of their various apartments for a bath, and that he had more than once remarked to her that he did not believe in using baths in apartment houses which other people had access to. At the trial, it will be noted, under the encouraging suggestions of Mr. Marshall Hall, she was disposed to magnify somewhat the passion which ranks next to godliness, so far as it moved Mr. Smith.

About June, 1909, Smith was in Southampton with Miss Pegler, and using his customary licence of wandering forth o' nights without her, he encountered Miss S—— A—— F——. Posing as George Rose, bachelor and dealer in antiques, he laid immediate siege to her heart, but for a time they did not meet. In October he renewed his protestations; after a fortnight, during which he made play with the mythical moneyed and mysterious resources in the bank, of which, needless to say, Miss F—— saw nothing, she capitulated, and they were married on October 29 at the local register office by special licence. The rest of Miss F——'s story is soon told.

They took the train to Clapham Junction, and put their belongings in the cloakroom, while they went to find apartments. "Mr. Rose" knew that his inamorata had £50 in cash before he married her, and he lost little time in ascertaining the full extent of her resources; he looked at her bank-book while she was unpacking, and was delighted to find that she was worth £260, without including about £30 of Government stock. By November 2 or 3 the whole £260 in notes and gold—he had asked for it all in gold—was in Mr. Rose's possession—he denying to his yielding bride the price of a taxi fare. She had already given him the £50. On November 5 the proceeds of the sale of the Government stock were handed over to Mr. Rose in his

wife's presence, and, having now acquired everything but
what she stood up in, the antique dealer and picture restorer
was moved by a' very natural desire to expand his bride's
mind (as he was soon to enlarge her knowledge of human
nature) by taking her to the National Gallery. Here, by a
coincidence which befell him again in Miss Reavil's case,
Mr. Smith was obliged to retire and leave his submissive
lady, promising to return in a moment. He did return—to
their lodgings, where he packed up every stick of clothing
the poor, deceived and betrayed girl possessed, and when,
after waiting an hour at the Gallery, she returned to their
apartments, she found only three empty boxes and his cycle,
which was left in the cloakroom. As in Miss Reavil's case,
he sent a lying letter and a further registered letter. Miss
F——, with but a few pence left in the world, went to a
friend's house for the night, and never saw Mr. Rose again
until he was in custody on a charge of murder, on April 24,
1915.

Smith, true to his invariable practice, now rejoined Miss
Pegler, he writing to her to meet him at Southend. On
November 16 he invested £240 of Miss F——'s fortune in
buying 22 Glenmore Street, Southend, the price of which
was £270, £30 remaining on mortgage. During his visit to
the Gallery he had doubtless gazed at the masterpieces of
our greatest land and seascape painter, and he told his
confiding Edith that the funds he had so surprisingly
become possessed of represented a fortunate deal in a
seascape by Joseph Mallord William Turner.

After leaving Southend, the Smiths went to Ashley Down
Road, Bristol, where he resided, maintaining himself on
further loans until September 2, 1910, when the amount
owing was about £93. He was still borrowing on the
Southend house, for he sent a receipt for a loan received
from the Woolwich Equitable Building Society, from which
he had purchased the property.

Smith was now nearing the end of his resources, and he
proceeded to search for another dupe. In the neighbour-

hood of Clifton—perhaps in those charming Leigh Woods dear to the memory of every old Cliftonian—he encountered Beatrice Constance Annie Mundy. She was the daughter of a deceased bank manager, and was at the time thirty-three years of age. Soon after her father's death her relatives persuaded her to execute a voluntary settlement of her property acquired under her father's will; her fortune amounted to some £2,500 in gilt-edged securities. Smith soon won Miss Mundy's confidence and affection, and they became engaged after a few days' acquaintance. He arrived on August 22 with Miss Mundy at 14 Rodwell Avenue, Weymouth, where they took two rooms, and on the 26th they were married at the register office, he giving the name of Henry Williams, thirty-five, bachelor, picture restorer, son of Henry John Williams, commercial traveller. Miss Mundy, of course, gave correct particulars.

"Mr Williams" was prompt in discovering that his bride received her income monthly from her trustees at the rate of £8 a month, and that there was due to her some £138, which they retained in hand to meet emergencies. On the very wedding day we find him instructing a Mr. Wilkinson, solicitor, of Messrs. Wilkinson & Eaton, Weymouth, to write to Mr. Ponting, the Mundy family solicitor, of Warminster, for a copy of the late bank manager's will. He then discovered the existence of the settlement, which protected the *corpus* of the property from his grasp; but still he could procure the £138, and he took the most energetic steps to obtain it. By September 13, he had possession of all the accumulated arrears in gold, less about £3 for Mr. Eaton's professional charges. He at once absconded, leaving Miss Mundy penniless, and almost without clothing, and he wrote her the cruel and disgusting letter which was read by Mrs. Crabbe, the landlady, in her evidence, and in which he accused his temporary paramour of disease and immorality—both accusations, needless to say, were quite unfounded.

He returned to Miss Pegler, and arranged to pay off his

debt to the Equitable, writing from Ashley Down Road, and on September 21 he called at the office and paid off the £93 mortgage. To account for his absence at Weymouth, he told his faithful Edith that he had "been to London and round the country." The pair did not stop long at Bristol, but moved to an address in Southend—not Glenmore Road—where they took premises and set up a small antique and general dealer's shop. There they remained for about four months, going thence to Barking Road, to Walthamstow, and once more to Bristol, Smith carrying on in each place the same sort of business in antiques. It was early in 1912 that they set up in Bristol, at Bath Road, Brislington.

For seven weeks life ran on uneventfully for Miss Pegler, when her husband began to show symptoms of restlessness. He said he would go to London and round the country dealing. He accordingly left her, with very little money, to run the small shop during his five months of absence, writing on the few occasions when he did write from the Woolwich Equitable Society's address. As Smith did not support her—he sent her only £2 in five months—and the business was not a thriving one, Miss Pegler sold it for a few pounds (about £5) and returned to her mother at 102 Ashley Down Road. When she next saw her husband she beheld the murderer of Beatrice Mundy.

By what the police believe to be the only genuine coincidence in the case, the errant footsteps of Smith took him in March to Weston-super-Mare, where Beatrice Mundy had been stopping since February 2 at the house of Mrs. Tuckett, a boarding-house named Norwood. I will give the story of the reunion of "Mr. and Mrs. Williams" in Mrs. Tuckett's own words. On March 14 Miss Mundy went out about eleven to buy some flowers for Mrs. Tuckett, who expected her back in half an hour. She, in fact, returned at one. "She said"—I quote Mrs. Tuckett—"as soon as she went out she found her husband looking over the sea. She was very excited." At three he arrived. I shall dwell

later on the instantly unfavourable impression he made on
Mrs. Tuckett. The following passage is from her examination-in-chief:

MR. BODKIN: After these questions that you put to the
prisoner did he leave?

MRS. TUCKETT: I told him it was my duty to wire to her
aunt.

MR. BODKIN: And did he remain in the house that
night?

MRS. TUCKETT: Oh no. She went with him. She said,
"I suppose I may go with my husband?" I said, "I cannot
hold you back; you are thirty!" She was over thirty; thirty-
one or thirty-two. She left with him. She never took anything with her. In fact she had promised me to come back
that night. I did not see her again.

Apparently it was not only the good Mrs. Tuckett who
read the sinister mind of the man, for in the letter of
March 15 he refers to the "heated arguments which would
have occurred if my wife and self had to face you and
your friends this evening."

Incidentally he bilked Mrs. Tuckett of about £2 10s.,
but any annoyance she felt at this was probably removed
by the compliment the judge paid her at the Central
Criminal Court three years later.

MR. JUSTICE SCRUTTON: I am obliged to you, Mrs.
Tuckett, for the clear and audible way you have given your
evidence.

The next move of "Mr. Williams" was to get into touch
with his wife's relations—with a view to an ostensible
reconciliation and the extraction of more money. He
accordingly dragged the submissive lady to the office of
Mr. Lillington, of Messrs. Baker & Co., solicitors, of
Waterloo Street. The visit was paid on the very day of
the apparently accidental meeting! With extraordinary
effrontery Mr. Williams proceeded, in his wife's hearing,
to give a totally untrue account of the circumstances under
which he had decamped with her money in August, 1910.

He professed, too, to have "borrowed" £150 from her to repay a loan, and, on the solicitor's suggestion, he gave his wife a note for that sum, with interest at 4 per cent. Mr. Lillington, perceiving that Mr. Williams was doing all the talking and that the wife was "in an assenting demeanour," challenged her as to the truth of every one of the husband's statements, and in every instance she confirmed them. He strongly advised her to send the promissory note to her uncle, but, of course, Mr. Williams frustrated any such intention. When Mr. Lillington saw them for the second and last time on March 16, Mrs. Williams still had the note at their lodgings—and it never turned up again.

Leaving Weston-super-Mare, this singular couple travelled about, staying at lodgings in different towns, and late in May they left Ashley and came to Herne Bay. Here on May 20, "Bluebeard of the Bath," as Mr. George R. Sims has dubbed him, walked into the house of Mr. F. H. Wilbee, J.P., of that town, a considerable owner of small house property there. Within that house was a little office where, at rather a high desk, there sat and had been sitting for thirty-six and a half years Miss Carrie Esther Rapley. He did not know it—this cheap *accapareur de femmes* with the appearance of a butcher and the breeding of a scavenger—but he had met one of those women, and there were several in the case, whose feminine instinct, like the protective antennæ of insects, warned them that here was a dangerous man. Miss Rapley was not a young woman, but because she was a woman, Smith, without any friendships or even acquaintanceships among men, immediately proceeded to become expansive. I will let her admirably clear evidence speak for itself, only regretting that I cannot give it word for word. She becomes suspicious at the first interview. She asks for a banker's reference, and he produces a Savings Bank book. She asks to see it; he puts it back in his pocket. He is evasive about his means; but his wife has money. "I might just as well tell you she is a notch above me," and he grows more expansive. In the end he takes the house he had come to inquire about, 80 High Street, on a yearly tenancy, at £18 a year, rent payable monthly. The agreement calls for little comment; it was, however, a yearly tenancy; Mr. Williams wanted a monthly one, and he gave up the house, after paying two months' rent in advance, the second payment being at that singular interview with Miss Rapley which we shall come to later.

It will be recalled that soon after the marriage Mr. Williams became aware of his wife's voluntary settlement; he had already obtained a copy of this about September 5, 1910, but he obtained another later, through her, about June 10, 1912, and this he brought to the office of Mr. Annesley, solicitor, of Herne Bay, on June 18. That he was in need of raising money at once appears from the evidence of Mr. Hudgell, clerk to the Woolwich Equitable's solicitor, who produced a letter asking for the money due on the sale of the Southend house, "as it is very urgently required"; the letter bore the date May 12. A copy of the voluntary settlement was laid before Mr. G. F. Spear, of the Inner Temple, to advise. Mr. Williams, in short, wanted to know how he could get hold of the *corpus* of the wife's property. The trustees were very unlikely to consent to a revocation of the settlement in the circumstances; they were far from unlikely to exercise their discretion in buying the wife an annuity; if she died intestate, her estate would go to the next-of-kin under the Statute of Distributions, and the husband would get nothing; but if she, with £2,500, left a will in his favour, and he, without a shilling, executed a similar will in her favour, and she died? Counsel's opinion came back on July 2; it was Bessie Mundy's death warrant.

The mutual wills were drawn up by Mr. Annesley and executed by the parties on July 8. Next day Mr. Williams came to the shop of Mr. Hill, ironmonger, and "cheapened" a £2 bath down to £1 17s. 6d.; he did not pay for it, but returned it on July 15. Its dimensions were later carefully

taken by Detective-Inspector Neil. It may here be said that
it had no taps or fixings at all; it had to be filled and
emptied by hand, and the inspector found exactly how many
pails would be needed and how long it would take to carry
them from the kitchen to the fatal room in order to fill that
bath.

On the next day after that purchase Mr. Williams took
his wife to Dr. French, who had been qualified about two
years, and had set up in practice at Herne Bay, saying that
she had had a fit. Being unaware of the symptoms of
epileptic or any other fits, Mr. Williams prudently forbore
to enter into particulars, and Dr. French put him "leading
questions," which enabled him to recall just what the
doctor suggested and no more—limbs twitching, jaws moving, and so on; there was no suggestion of the dreadful
scream which almost invariably heralds an epileptic seizure
(as distinct from the *petit mal*), and Mr. Williams said no
word about a scream. The doctor prescribed bromide of
potassium, a useful general sedative, a specific in epilepsy
and an anaphrodisiac. In answer to the doctor's questions,
Mrs. Williams did not recollect anything about a fit; she
had never had any, and only complained of a headache.

On Friday, July 12, Williams fetched Dr. French to see
his wife in bed. The doctor saw nothing amiss, except
that her hands were clammy, the weather being very hot,
heart normal, tongue not very clean, face a little flushed;
she looked like one awakened from sleep on a hot night.
The doctor prescribed more bromide. At 3 p.m. he saw
the pair again, when Mrs. Williams looked "in perfect
health"; she complained of nothing worse than lassitude,
the weather being so hot. Before she went to bed that
night she wrote the following letter to her uncle, which she
registered. It was produced by him at the trial.

Last Tuesday night I had a bad fit, and one again on
Thursday night. It has left me weak and suffering from
nerves and headache, and has evidently shaken my whole

system. My husband has been extremely kind and done all he could for me. He has provided me with the attention of the best medical man here, who is constantly giving me medical treatment, and visiting me day and night.

I do not like to worry you with this, but my husband has strictly advised me to let all my relatives know and tell them of my breakdown. I have made out my will and have left all I have to my husband. That is only natural, as I love my husband.

At 8 a.m. next morning—Saturday July 13[1]—Dr. French was handed a note. It ran, "Can you come at once? I am afraid my wife is dead." The doctor hurried round to 80 High Street and found the door ajar; he entered and went upstairs with Williams, and saw Mrs. Williams lying on her back in the bath. Particulars of her position will be found elsewhere in the narrative. Her head was beneath the water, and on removing her body the doctor found that the pulse had ceased to beat; the body was not yet cold, but all attempts at restoration proved useless. A square piece of Castile soap was clutched in the right hand. Williams assisted the doctor while he was trying artificial respiration by holding the woman's tongue, her false teeth having been removed. The face was dusky and congested with blood. Finding her beyond human aid, Dr. French left the house, and about 10 a.m. Police Constable Kitchingham arrived, and saw the body lying quite naked; he also saw the bath three-parts full. He took a statement from Williams and went away. Williams now went out to arrange for the laying out of the body, and he first approached Mrs. Millgate, with whom he afterwards boarded, and who lived next door. She said that she was too busy to come,

[1] All these brides died on a Friday night or a Saturday morning. Alice Burnham on Friday night, December 12, 1913, and Margaret Lofty on Friday night, December 18, 1914. The convenience of holding the inquest before the relatives could attend need hardly be pointed out.

but at 2 p.m. she called at 80 High Street, and learning
from Williams that the woman the doctor was to send had
not come, she went upstairs with him. What then happened
I give in her own words:

MR. BODKIN: What room did you go into?

MRS. MILLGATE: The middle bedroom; and he said,
"She is in there." He stayed outside on the landing and
I went in, and I said, "In here." And I went in, and not
seeing anything but the bath, I looked behind the door,
and I saw Mrs. Williams lying on the floor quite naked.

MR. BODKIN: Quite naked?

MRS. MILLGATE: Yes; that gave me a great shock, and
I started back and turned suddenly round and said, "Oh
dear, it is not covered over." And he looked frightened as
I started back. Mr. Williams looked frightened as I started
back.

MR. BODKIN: Did you then cover the body up?

MRS. MILLGATE: Yes; I went back again into the room,
and I noticed she was lying on the edge of a sheet, and a
lot of it was to her feet, and I picked it up and covered over
the body. . . . I asked him to fetch me a pillow, just to
put under her head, as her head was on the bare floor, and
he said to me . . .

Here the witness, who was rather deaf, was interrupted,
and she did not give her reply. In her evidence at the police
court she spoke of seeing blood near the corpse's waist.
The medico-legal aspect of this I shall deal with at a
further stage. Williams had early in the morning asked
Mr. Millgate for "a few pieces of rag for the woman to
wipe up some blood." Alice Minter, who actually laid out
the body about 4 p.m., asked for "just the usual things—
nightdress, brush and comb, bath sponge, and a towel."

Whatever the explanation of the blood, it was Williams
who wiped it up.

Mr. Rutley Mowll, solicitor, of Dover, and coroner for
East Kent, was informed of the death on the day it occurred
by the police—probably by Kitchingham, who was coroner's

officer. He was for holding his inquest forthwith, but he found the inquest could not be conveniently taken that day, so he gave directions to hold it at 4.30 p.m. on the Monday. The Mundy family had heard by wire from Williams of the death that Saturday morning, very shortly after receiving the last letter from Bessie, which has been set out. The wire ran, "Bessie died in a fit this morning; letter following.—Williams."

On the Monday, Herbert Mundy received a letter from Williams. "Words cannot describe the great shock I suffered in the loss of my wife," wrote the bereaved husband. No word was breathed by him as to the holding of any inquest, nor as to the date of it. When Herbert Mundy next heard, "Crowner's Quest Law" had done its best—or worst—and Mr. Mowll, displaying, as he said, "more than ordinary perspicacity" and having "taken very great care," and having "thoroughly and carefully thrashed out" the case, returned through his jury a verdict that "the cause of her death was that while taking a bath she had an epileptic seizure, causing her to fall back into the water of the bath and be drowned, and so the jurors say that the said deceased died from misadventure."

The more than ordinary perspicacity of the coroner enabled him to state that, "assuming the husband was fond of his wife—and there was no evidence to the contrary, but a great deal of evidence that he was—it was a terrible plight." (I may pause to remark that Mr. Williams had shed copious crocodile tears during the inquest, as next day he did over Miss Rapley's desk, but in the case of that shrewd lady the simulation of great grief was not successfully attempted.) Mr. Mowll went on to say that "a request had been made to have a post-mortem, and if he had had the request earlier—he had it by the earliest possible moment the Mundy family could make it—he should then with an abundance of caution have requested the doctor to make an examination."

The first the Mundy family heard of any inquest was in

a letter from Mr. Williams, dated July 15, the day of the inquest, running:

> DEAR SIR,—I hope you received my letter this morning. The result of the inquest was misadventure by a fit in the bath. The burial takes place to-morrow at 2 p.m. I am naturally too sad to write any more to-day.

On the Sunday, July 14, the dead woman's brother, G. H. Mundy, wrote two letters, one to Williams, the other to the coroner. They were substantially the same, but not identical; and the purpose of them was this, "As Bessie's brother, I must insist that, as she died so suddenly, a post-mortem examination must be held before she is buried, for the satisfaction of all the family. Please see that this is carried out."

Whatever the minute discrepancies between Mr. Howard Mundy's letter to Williams and his letter to the coroner may have been, the coroner saw no reason to afford the Mundy family time to attend the inquest. The coroner and Williams compared their letters, and the result was that only Smith, *alias* Williams, *alias* Love, *alias* James, *alias* Baker, *alias* Lloyd, and Dr. French—a Herne Bay practitioner of two years' standing, strangely described by his patient as "the best medical man here, who is constantly giving me medical treatment"—gave the evidence upon which the verdict recorded was returned. The funeral was carried out by Mr. Hogbin, who had also provided the furniture for 80 High Street. "It was to be moderately carried out at an expense of seven guineas."

MR. BODKIN: And a grave?

MR. HOGBIN: He said he would not purchase a grave. The grave was 8s. 6d., the interment fee.

The funeral, which had been provisionally fixed to take place on Tuesday July 16, took place as arranged, as the inquest had gone "favourably," and two days later Smith resold to the undertaker the piano and other furniture at

80 High Street for £20 4s. On the morning of the funeral, timed for 2.30 p.m., the bereaved husband walked into Miss Rapley's office, and, putting his arms and head on her high desk, he began to sob. "She is dead," he groaned. "My wife; she had a fit during the week. I went out; she went to have a bath, and she must have had another fit, for when I came back I found her dead in the bath." Miss Rapley was too shocked to make any comment, so Mr. Williams proceeded, "Was it not a jolly good job I got her to make a will?" Miss Rapley was more shocked. Mr. Williams became angry. "Well, is it not the correct thing when people marry for the wife to make her will and leave everything to her husband, and for him to make his and leave everything to her?" he snorted. "Did you make yours?" asked Miss Rapley. "Yes," said Williams. "I then looked him very straight in the face and I said," so testified Miss Rapley, "I thought you told me you had not got anything?" "Oh, well, I made my will all the same," was the weak reply.

He then told Miss Rapley of the previous day's inquest—the first she had heard of it. She persisted, "Did you let her relatives know?" "Yes, I did, and the brutes sent a letter to the coroner saying it was a very suspicious case." Still Miss Rapley persisted, "Let me see, where did you say her relatives lived?" "I never told you where they lived," snapped Mr. Williams. Miss Rapley saw him once more at Herne Bay; he had come to pay the second and last instalment of rent; incidentally, he wanted her to find him a nice little place in the country—not more than £400. When she next saw Mr. Williams he was in custody on three charges of murder.

On July 17 Mr. Williams called on Mr. Annesley, the solicitor who had drawn up the wills, and instructed him to obtain probate of his wife's will. A caveat was lodged by the Mundy family about the end of July, but was withdrawn by Ponting & Co. on August 8, and in the course of the autumn of 1912 all the securities covered by the settlement (with the exception of £300 Cape of Good Hope stock retained until early in the following year against a liability of the estate for unpaid calls on shares in a moribund company) were handed over to Mr. Williams. His exact dealings with the Mundy securities, which he turned into gold and notes and then into house property, and then again into cash and finally into an annuity, were traced in minute detail by Detective-Inspector Neil. Many different banking accounts were used by Smith all over the south and west of England, and he obtained by receipts £2,403 15s. against payments of £2,042 9s. 5d. The correspondence in relation to the winding-up of Mrs. Williams' estate, carried on between Mr. Annesley, Messrs. Ponting, Smith, and others, is contained in no less than 215 letters and telegrams; the professional letters are very much like others, but the personal ones of Smith, from their spelling, style, and persistent inquiries after money, are very idiosyncratic.

Probate was granted about September 11. Illness in the Mundy family and delays caused by Smith's own interference rendered the negotiations somewhat protracted, and "Mr. Williams" was very reluctant to pay Mr. Annesley's bill, or to furnish Messrs. Ponting with any particulars about himself. Under date August 1, 1912, he writes to Annesley, "I was educated at Whitechurch, Glasgow (*sic*), after which I went to Canada—returned to London. I have always been of an extremely roaming disposition, never keeping a diary, but continually up and down the country buying and selling pictures, etc. I never remained in one particular town more than a week or so." On August 4 he writes, "Now, in regard to my history, which was requested by them, that also is bluff. It is not the matter of history inasmuch as the only proof required is whether I am the lawful husband of the deceased. If it was a matter of history, what on earth is the use of a will?"

The inspector was equally indefatigable in tracing the purchases and sales of house property. The net result was that Smith purchased the houses for £2,187 10s., and sold them for £1,455, a loss of over £600 in a few months. He invested £1,300 in an annuity in the North British and Mercantile Insurance Company, payable half-yearly in April and October, at a total charge of £76 1s. a year.

I will now pick up the threads of the story of Miss Pegler. That lady was never able to ascertain where her spouse resided when away from her. His rare letters came through the Woolwich Equitable or from some accommodation address. When he met her at Margate, as we shall presently see, and she told him that she had tried to find him at Woolwich and Ramsgate, he was very angry, and said he should never tell her his business again. He did not believe in women knowing his business and vehemently requested her to do no such thing again.

About the end of July or the beginning of August Miss Pegler received a letter from Smith asking her to join him at Margate; she did so. They stayed a week, and went on to Tunbridge Wells and other places mentioned in her evidence. She naturally asked him what he had been up to. He was angry, as has been said, but he condescended to inform her that he had just returned from Canada, where he had been very fortunate in buying a Chinese image for a song and selling it for £1,000. Mr. and Mrs. Smith appeared to have lived together for over a year, he leaving her early in October, 1913, to go round the country; he explained that he had to do some dealing, as he had dropped £600 over his houses. When he returned after his calculated murder of Alice Burnham, he said he had just come from Spain, where he had bought some old-fashioned jewellery, which brought him in £200 eventually.

A very singular incident had occurred just before Smith went away to marry and murder Alice Burnham. He made the acquaintance, in August or September, while they were at Weston-super-Mare, of a young woman of twenty-eight or thirty years of age, of the name of Burdett, as far as Miss Pegler could recollect. She was a governess, and Miss Pegler several times saw the boy and two girls she had in charge. Some intimacy developed, and the Smiths asked her to tea. She came about four times, sometimes bringing the children. Smith told his Edith that he was going to insure the young lady as an "investment," and an insurance agent actually called to discuss the matter, Smith taking Miss Burdett to see him. A policy for £500 was provisionally arranged. Miss Pegler, much against her inclination, accompanied Miss Burdett to see the insurance company's doctor, and Miss Burdett was passed as a first-class life. Miss Burdett knew quite well that the Smiths were married, and for some reason Smith cancelled the policy—if, indeed, it was ever issued—and recovered his premium.

When Smith left Miss Pegler he proceeded to Southsea, where he met Alice Burnham, his next victim, apparently at the chapel she attended. She was twenty-five years of age, and was nursing an old gentleman named Holt. She was a stout but healthy young woman, and had made a very good recovery from a somewhat serious operation. Within a very few days Smith had induced her to consent to an engagement. With that minute attention to matters of money so characteristic of him, "George" brought his bank books and private papers when he came to propose, and from what we know of him we may be sure he lost no time in ascertaining from his new flame exactly how her financial affairs stood.

On October 15 the deluded girl wrote to her people announcing her engagement, whilst Smith on October 22 wrote to Mrs. Burnham, Alice's mother, a letter expressing, in endearing terms, his affection for her daughter, and advising her that they were coming down to Aston Clinton to pay a visit. In accordance with the intention expressed in his letter, Smith and Alice Burnham journeyed to Aston Clinton, on Saturday October 25, and were met at Tring station by her father, with his pony and trap. They remained until October 31, the visit being cut short by the behaviour of Smith, which the family found so objectionable that Mr. Burnham asked his daughter to leave. Indeed, from the first Mr. Burnham felt the strongest dislike of Smith, whom he described as a man of "very evil appearance, so much so that he could not sleep whilst Smith was in the house, as he feared Smith was a bad man and that something serious would happen." Smith avoided Mr. Burnham as much as possible.

Notwithstanding the chilling hostility of the family, Alice and Smith gave notice of their intended marriage at the church at Aston Clinton. That intention, however, they abandoned, and, returning to Southsea, they were married on November 4 at the Portsmouth Register Office, he giving his true name, describing his age as forty, and his condition as bachelor, of independent means, son of George Thomas Smith, deceased, artist, flowers and figure.

It may here be noted that Mr. Burnham had inquired at Somerset House, but no trace of Smith's birth could be found.

Alice Burnham's means at the time of her marriage were these—in the Savings Bank, £27 19s. 5d.; due from her father £100 and interest on his promissory note; due from her sister, Mrs. Pinchin, £10. She had also a quantity of jewellery and clothing.

It is best to tell the story of what happened in Inspector Neil's own words, as giving the reader an example of an official narrative, which presents the main facts with a telling succinctness.

20/10/13   she drew all her money from the bank, £27 19s. 5d., and on

3/11/13   prisoner introduced her to Mr. Pleasance, an insurance agent, with the result that she was insured for £500. On the

4/11/13   the prisoner married her at Portsmouth Register Office in the name of George Joseph Smith. He immediately commenced application to Mr. Burnham for the £100, which Mr. Burnham declined to send as he was suspicious of the

man and desired to know something of his antecedents, and for this purpose consulted Mr.
Redhead, solicitor, of Aylesbury, who wrote to
the prisoner, asking him something about himself, and in reply Mr. Burnham received an
insulting postcard stating that his mother was
a cab horse, etc. Every obstacle was put in the
way of the money being sent, and the prisoner
threatened to commence proceedings. Mr. Burnham was eventually advised to part with the
money, and on

29/11/13   he forwarded £104 1s. 1d. to his solicitor, who
sent it on to the prisoner through his solicitor.
It is known that this money was paid by the
prisoner into his own banking account. On

4/12/13   the insurance on Miss Burnham's life was com-
pleted and the premium of £24 17s. 1d. paid.
This was no doubt the money drawn out of the
P.O. On

8/12/13   Miss Burnham called on Mr. March, solicitor,
Portsmouth, and made a will in favour of her
husband. On

10/12/13   prisoner and Miss Burnham went to Blackpool
and called on Mrs. Marsden at 35 Adelaide
Street, but declined to take rooms there as there
was no bath there, and they were recommended
to go to Regent's Road where they took lodgings
with Mrs. Crossley. The same day they called
on Dr. Billing where the prisoner explained that
his wife had a headache in consequence of a
train journey. She was prescribed for. On

11/12/13   Miss Burnham asked for a bath, which was
prepared by Mrs. Crossley, and shortly after
the prisoner went to Mrs. Crossley and said he
could not make his wife hear. She was found
dead in her bath by prisoner and Mrs. Crossley.
Dr. Billing was sent for, and on

13/12/13   an inquest was held and a verdict of death from drowning was returned. A funeral was arranged for to take place on

15/12/13   and on the day before Miss Burnham's mother and brother went to Blackpool to be present at the funeral. The same day Smith left them (immediately after the funeral) and said he had to get back to Portsmouth. They never saw him again though he promised to write. He went to 80 Kimberley Road, sold all Miss Burnham's belongings and then went to London where he approached Kingsbury & Turner, solicitors, Brixton, on

18/12/13   with a view to them obtaining probate. On

22/12/13   he returned to Miss Pegler at Bristol, when he said he had been to Spain and done fairly well. On the

19/1/14   he received the money from the insurance under Burnham's will through Heath & Eckersall, Cheltenham, to whom he had gone after Kingsbury & Turner had obtained probate. He resided in Cheltenham some time with Pegler. The money paid under the insurance was £506, and on

22/1/14   with this money he increased his annuity to the extent of £500. With Miss Pegler he then went back to Bristol.

Here for a time I will leave the Inspector and resume my narrative.

Smith had so completely estranged the affections and warped the mind of Alice Burnham during the brief period of their engagement that she actually brought herself to write two letters on November 22 and 24 to her father, in which she advised him on the former date that that was her last application for her £100 and interest on his promissory note, and finally on the 24th that she had instructed her solicitor to take "extreme measures to obtain the money you have in your possession." She also went so far as to instruct Mr. Robinson, a solicitor, to write to her married sister, Annie Pinchin, demanding the return of £10 which she had lent her; later on, however, on the sister's marriage, she told her to regard it as a gift. The £10 was repaid on November 28, by registered letter.

It is needless to anticipate the story of what happened at Blackpool; the medico-legal aspects are dealt with later. But one or two matters call for mention here, because the witnesses did not refer to them in their evidence.[1] On the afternoon following the murder of Alice Burnham, Smith returned with a full bottle of whisky; in the evening there was only a little drop left. He spent part of the afternoon playing the piano. He told Margaret Crossley that he had been in the Marines, and had shaved off his moustache a fortnight previously. He declined to pay the bill for the food supplied to Mrs. Burnham and her son. Mrs. Crossley had great difficulty in getting him to pay for his own board and lodging. He promised to recompense her for the trouble she had been put to, but he never did. To Joseph Crossley he said that he wanted a deal coffin, and on Crossley replying that he would not bury his wife like that, even if he had not a penny in the world, Smith retorted, "When they are dead they are done with."

A matter of some importance was noticed in Superintendent Wootton's letter from Aylesbury.

I desire to draw your attention to Smith's letter to Mrs. Burnham dated 13/12/13, giving an account of his wife's death, etc., in which he states that the inquest would be held early next week, whereas it was held on the day the letter was written.

In consequence of this deception, the second inquest was

[1] For complete evidence in the cases of Mundy, Burnham and Lofty see *Trial of George Joseph Smith*, Notable British Trials Series (Wm. Hodge & Co. Ltd., London).

of the same perfunctory character as the first. It was all over in half an hour, and many points of suspicion were never brought out—as that Valiant, the coroner's officer, noticed that the distracted "husband" had carefully removed his coat and rolled up his right shirt sleeve before raising his "bride's" head out of the water, and that Mrs. Haynes, who resided next door, had noticed a very considerable quantity of hair at the sloping end of the bath (the deceased had been sitting facing that end) on the Sunday morning, when she went to clean the bath.

Again, Smith was a transparently uneducated man. Yet his statement that, "I am a gentleman of independent means, and have never followed any occupation," aroused no incredulity—though he had told his very landlady that he had been a marine! The only witnesses were Dr. Billing, Mrs. M. Crossley, Valiant and another sergeant, and Smith himself. He duly contrived—assisted, maybe, by the bottle of whisky he had consumed—to make his lachrymal glands perform their function, and his freely flowing crocodile tears moved all hearts except Mrs. Crossley's.

The coroner had another inquest to hold and the 8 p.m. train to catch—all between 6.30 and 8, so with little ado the jurors of Our Lord the King found that "the deceased Alice Smith came to her death at Blackpool aforesaid on the 12th day of December, 1913. The deceased suffered from heart disease, and was found drowned in a hot bath, probably through being seized with a fit or faint. The cause of death was accidental."

The deception as to the letting off of the water in Smith's letter to Mrs. Burnham is truly remarkable. When Dr. Billing arrived on the scene he asked Smith why he had not lifted his wife out; he said he could not. He was then asked why he could not pull the plug; he said he never thought of it! And yet in the letter he says—"I held her head out of the water and let the water run off away from her; when the doctor came we lifted her out of the bath." His lying hypocrisy can be estimated even better when one reads that in the same letter he describes the death as "the greatest and most cruel shock that ever a man could have suffered."

Smith fled hastily from the scene of his crime. He left his address with Mrs. M. Crossley on a postcard. On the back she wrote, "Wife died in bath. We shall see him again." When the card was shown to her at the Old Bailey two years later, the usher was directed to show her and the jury only the address side of that card. What Mrs. Crossley wrote—like what the soldier said—was not evidence. As he sped down the street she hurled after him an opprobrious name—"Crippen."

With that sordid love of money which never forsook him, he realized all his wife's wardrobe and jewellery just as he had sold Bessie Mundy's linen to a Margate dealer before Mrs. Millgate, his landlady, had got it back from the laundry.

He returned to Edith Pegler, and with her recommenced those aimless wanderings from place to place—Bournemouth, Torquay, etc., until about August 14, when, once more in Bournemouth, he marked down his penultimate victim in the person of Alice Reavil, a domestic servant.

She gave evidence at Bow Street, and her statement, as taken by Inspector Cole and P. S. Page, reads as follows:

On 7th or 8th September I was in the garden on the front, sitting on a seat, when a man came and spoke to me. . . . We had some conversation, in which he said he admired my figure. After an hour's conversation, in which he informed me he was an artist, and had £2 a week from some land in Canada, he made an appointment for 6 p.m. the same evening. I met him as arranged; he did not tell me where he was staying; I never knew. Next day I met him as arranged, and he then told me his name was "Charles Oliver James." He said he had been to Canada and his agents sent him his money. He also said he understood I had some money. I met him every evening, and I returned to Woolwich on the 14th or 15th September. After the third or fourth day of our acquaintance he asked me to marry him, and I consented, and he said he would put his money with mine and he would open an antique shop. . . . He asked me how much money I had, and I said about £70 odd, and some furniture, including a piano. He asked me to sell them, and I decided to. . . . We went to the Register Office and were married by special licence [this was on September 17]. In the meantime I had sold my belongings, and they realized £14. After we married we left Woolwich for Waterloo, and went to 8 Hafer Road, Battersea Rise, where he had taken two furnished rooms. . . . On the way he showed me a lot of bank-notes, and he asked me for my £14 to put in the bank with his. I gave it to him. When we got to our lodgings . . . he produced a Post Office withdrawal form for me to fill up to draw all my money from the bank. I filled it up, and added, "with interest to close account," and we went out together to post it. . . . He put it in the box. I signed the withdrawal form in my maiden name, and he gave instructions to the landlady to take it in. . . . About three days later the warrant for withdrawal was delivered, and he took it in. This was on Saturday, September 19, 1914. He kept the warrant. All my clothing was at this address, and was kept in four boxes. On September 21 we went to the Post Office, Lavender Hill, to obtain the money. . . . He told me to ask for all £1 notes, but they gave me four £10 notes and two £5 notes, and the remainder in £1 notes and cash. In all I received £75 6s. and some coppers. He picked up the notes and I the cash—the odd 6s. I never saw the notes again. . . . The same evening we packed our belongings, with the intention of getting another house. He went out to get a man to take the luggage to Clapham station, and later a man arrived with a barrow to take it away—as I thought, to the station. . . . He told the landlady we should go away next day;

he paid the bill—I think 10s.; I had bought all the food
we had. On September 22 we left the house. . . . We
got on a tram-car, and on the way he spoke of Halifax,
Nova Scotia, and asked me if I would like to go. He took
penny fares and we got off at some gardens. We walked
through the gardens and on getting to the other end he
said he was going to the lavatory and asked me to wait.
I did so, and waited about an hour. He did not return
so I returned to 8 Hafer Road, and found the attached
telegram waiting for me. [It ran, "Wait home for letter.
Next post—James."] I remained as requested and some
hours later received a letter (registered), posted at Battersea. I stayed at Hafer Road the same night, and returned
to 39 Plumstead Common Road next day. None of my
boxes arrived, and I have not seen them since. On
February 22 . . . I attended Bow Street, and I identified a man known as George Smith as my husband.
. . . I communicated with the Post Office, and obtained
the numbers of the notes paid on the warrant. When I
married the prisoner he was clean-shaven. I value my
clothing, jewellery, etc., at about £50. The result of my
meeting with prisoner was that I was left with only a few
shillings and the clothes I was actually wearing. What
he had taken consisted of the whole of my life savings.

Smith now for the last time rejoined Edith Pegler, taking
with him Alice Reavil's modest trousseau. This—or,
rather, what remained of it—he gave to her, remarking
that "he had been to a sale in London and had bought
some lady's clothing. He had some left, and gave it to me.
It was kept in a black trunk, which I had not seen before.
The lady's clothing taken away by the police was brought
to Weston-super-Mare by Smith."

During the period between the Reavil marriage and the
Lofty murder, Miss Pegler thought about November 1914.
"He remarked to me that, if I interfered with his business,
I should never have another happy day, as the world was

wide, and he would forfeit it all. This was because I had spoken about his annuity. Just after Christmas 1914, we were living in apartments at 10 Kennington Avenue, Bristol, and I said I was going to have a bath. He said, ' In that bath there? '—referring to the bathroom—' I should advise you to be careful of those things, as it is known that women often lose their lives through weak hearts and fainting in a bath.' "

Towards the end of 1914 the Smiths were in Bristol, when a mood of restlessness once more swept over George Joseph, and he said he "would have a run round again before Christmas with another 'young fellow'—he had met in Clifton." The "young fellow" was Margaret Elizabeth Lofty, spinster, aged thirty-eight, daughter of the late Rev. Fitzroy Fuller Lofty, who had died in 1892, leaving a widow, one son and three daughters. Miss Lofty soon responded to Smith's overtures; a disappointment in love a year before —it turned out that the man had a wife already—had rather unsettled her for her vocation as companion to elderly ladies in quiet cathedral cities; and Smith, whatever he lacked in address or education, left nothing to be desired from the point of uxoriousness or virility. She seems to have perceived that her mother and sisters would be critical of her *fiancé*; so she writes them pious untruths; she is going away to be clandestinely married, and she writes, under date December 15, 1914, Bristol station—

DEAR ELSIE,—I am off to a situation and meet my lady here. We go, I believe, to London for a day or two. Don't worry. . . . Your affectionate sister,—PEGGY.

And she encloses a note for her mother in similar vein— all untrue.

As she had but about £19 in the Savings Bank, a life policy became imperatively necessary from Smith's point of view. He is "John Lloyd" now. He has ceased to be of independent means, and has become a land agent, like his father before him, one John Arthur Lloyd. Accordingly, the unsuspecting victim is sent to the office of the Yorkshire Insurance Company, 4 St. Stephen's Avenue, Bristol. She did not strike Mr. Cooper, of that office, as at all a good business woman when he first saw her on November 24. She called again next day, and filled in a proposal form for a £700 endowment policy. One regrets to note that she told several untruths when applying; it is needless to suggest who inspired them. She said she was of independent means, whereas she had but £19 odd; she said that she did not contemplate matrimony, whereas she was bent on nothing else; she said that she had brought her birth certificate because Mr. Cooper had suggested it, whereas he had done no such thing; the question of proving her age had never been mentioned by him. She wished the issue of the policy to be expedited as much as possible, and the insurance was completed on December 4, when she paid the premium, no doubt with money supplied by Smith —it was in the form of new Treasury notes obtained from the unfortunate Alice Reavil—because she had not enough of her own in the bank. She struck Mr. Cooper as having learnt a good deal—" had the business at her finger-ends " —about insurance matters since her first visit, and he thought she must have been prompted by someone.

On December 17 the parties were married, Smith of the occupation of land agent and in the name of John Lloyd, aged thirty-eight, his bride of the same age; she gave, of course, a correct account of her parentage. They left Dalkeith House, 4 Stanley Road, Bath, from which they had been married, the same day, and, with no luggage beyond a hold-all and a gladstone bag, took the train to London, and went to 16 Orchard Road, Highgate, where Lloyd had booked rooms on the previous Monday, paying 6s. deposit. The house was owned by a Miss Lokker, and a Mrs. Heiss managed it in her absence; there were reasons why they had to be especially careful, in 1915, and that they did not take in undesirable lodgers without references;

in fact, they had had such lodgers, and they had been
robbed. The facts were that Miss Lokker was a Dutch
subject and Mrs. Heiss a German. At Bow Street Mrs.
Heiss stated, "I did not like the way he asked about the
bath."

Lloyd, when he called on the Monday, had asked to see
the bath. He looked at it "as if he was measuring it with
his eyes," and said to Mrs. Heiss, "This is rather a small
bath, but I dare say it is large enough for someone to lie
in." He looked at her and smiled, and she said, "It is." He
decided to take the rooms, paid his deposit, and left. But
he had made so bad an impression by his manner that
Miss Lokker had decided by Thursday that she would not
let him the rooms. When he arrived with his bride, about
3 p.m. on that day, the door was opened to him by a
Mr. Van Rhym, who said, "You cannot have the rooms
now; they are not ready," and told him to return at 6 p.m.
Lloyd appeared annoyed and nasty, and left his luggage in
the passage and went away. Detective-Sergeant Dennison
had so advised when he visited the house at 2.30, at Miss
Lokker's request; he had acted for her in the matter of
the other undesirable lodgers. Lloyd returned a little after
5 p.m., but Mrs. Heiss was so frightened by his evil appearance that she would not let him in; he kept knocking and
calling out to people in the road that, if it were not for his
wife, he would have knocked the man (Mr. Van Rhym)
down.

Dennison had arranged to call again at six, and Miss
Lokker, in some alarm, went through a neighbour's house
to look for him. Lloyd was at the door. "He was in a
temper, and asked me if I had anything to do with the
house. I said 'No.' He said a lot I do not remember, but
I know I asked if he had given a reference. He said, 'I
have never heard of such a thing. I have plenty of money
and a banker; that is good enough.' He said he had been
everywhere abroad, but had never been treated as he was
being treated. He said 'I can see it is all planned. All I

want is my money and luggage back; I have taken rooms somewhere else.' He did not know I was the landlady, and all the time he was talking to me he was running the place down."

At six o'clock Dennison opened the door to Mr. and Mrs. Lloyd, and said, "You cannot have the rooms, because you cannot furnish references." In reply to Lloyd's question, "Who are you?" the officer cautiously replied, "I am acting on behalf of the landlady." Mr. Lloyd turned to his bride, exclaimed, "They don't want us," and having been given back his deposit, was shown the door by the detective; he departed in a passion.

Mr. Lloyd sought apartments next at 14 Bismarck Road, Highgate (now Waterloo Road), where Miss Blatch had a furnished room to let. He came with his bride, without luggage, paid seven shillings deposit, and went away, as he said, to fetch the luggage. Before agreeing to take the room, Mrs. Lloyd had inquired if there was a bath; the answer was in the affirmative. During her husband's absence, Mrs. Lloyd told Miss Blatch that she did not know her husband's plans, but they were going to Scotland for their honeymoon. It is needless to travel in detail over the evidence of the witnesses as to the death at Bismarck Road. I will condense the narrative in the Inspector's style. About 5 p.m. on

17/12/14   Smith in the name of Lloyd arrives at 14 Bismarck Road, and takes a room after inquiring if there is a bath, and at 8 p.m., on

17/12/14   he takes "Mrs. Lloyd" to see Dr. Bates at 30 Archway Road, who prescribes for her, and on

18/12/14   Mrs. Lloyd goes to the office of Mr. Lewis, solicitor, 84 High Street, Islington, and makes her will, bequeathing everything to her husband, who was appointed sole executor. On the same day she draws out her whole balance in the savings bank from Muswell Hill Post Office, £19 9s. 5d., having given notice of withdrawal on the fifteenth, and on

18/12/14 she returns to Bismarck Road, and at 7.30 p.m. on

18/12/14 Mrs. Lloyd asks for a hot bath, and at 8.15 p.m. on

18/12/14 P.C. Heath is called to the house and he finds Mrs. Lloyd dead, and on

20/12/14 Mr. Lloyd calls on Mrs. Beckett and desires to have the funeral next day, and on

22/12/14 Mr. Schroder holds an inquest, which he adjourns to

1/1/15 when the jury finds that Mrs. Lloyd died from suffocation by drowning in the water, Mr. Dale, instructed by Mr. Aylwin, appearing for Lloyd, and on

4/1/15 Smith, as John Lloyd, calls on Mr. W. P. Davies, solicitor, of 60 Uxbridge Road, Shepherd's Bush, and produces the will of Mrs. Lloyd, *née* Lofty, and her marriage certificate and her life policy and instructs him to obtain probate. On

19/1/15 in consequence of information received, Detective-Inspector Neil communicates with the Aylesbury police and with the G.P.O., and on

21/1/15 Inspector Wootton replies from Aylesbury, and reports are received the same day from Bath and Bristol. On

22/1/15 three documents reach the police, Mrs. Lloyd's bank book, her withdrawal order, and receipt for £19 9s. 5d., and on

22/1/15 Inspector Neil submits his first report, subject "Suspicious deaths," from Kentish Town, and on

1/2/15 having kept daily observation on Mr. Davies's premises the police see Mr. Lloyd enter the office. On leaving he is stopped by Detective-

Inspector Neil and Police-Sergeants Page and
Reed, when he admits he is also George Smith,
who married Alice Burnham, who died in her
bath at Blackpool. "As it was thought he
might be in possession of fire-arms he was
searched but none were found." He was not
dressed in mourning, and the only evidence of
such found was a black tie in his bedroom at
his new address—14 Richmond Road—where
was found a hold-all with a quantity of ladies'
clothing. Lloyd was identified as Smith the same
night by Mr. Burnham and Mrs. Pinchin, and on

2/2/15   he is charged with causing a false entry to be
made in the marriage register at Bath. (It was
false not only as to his name, etc., but as to
his and his wife's period of residence in Bath
previous to the marriage.) He is remanded at
Bow Street and on

23/3/15   he is further charged with the wilful murder of
Bessie Mundy, Alice Burnham, and Margaret
Lofty, and after several remands is committed
on all three charges on

12/5/15   and on

9/6/15   a true bill is returned against him at Lancaster
Assizes for the murder of Alice Burnham, and
on

15/6/15   a true bill is returned at the Central Criminal
Court in respect of Miss Lofty. On

16/6/15   a true bill is returned at Maidstone in respect
of Miss Mundy, and the two country indictments
are removed to the C.C.C. under "Palmer's
Act."

Alice Reavil alone of the women defrauded and deserted
gave evidence during the proceedings at Bow Street. Smith,
on almost every occasion, lost all command over himself,
hurling imprecations at Inspector Neil and Mr. Bodkin,

who appeared for the Crown and was reviled by the man in the dock as a "criminal and a manufacturer of criminals." Mrs. Crossley was, as at the Old Bailey, denounced as a lunatic. After the prisoner's committal, Mr. Montague Shearman apologized for his client's outbreaks, but he behaved little better on his trial until a withering rebuke from the judge put an end to his ill-timed and ill-bred interruptions, betraying, as they did, the wreckage of his nervous system, the not unnatural consequence of forty-three years of life mis-spent in crime and debauchery.

As some little mystery has prevailed as to the manner in which Scotland Yard was first put on the track of the murderer, it may be said that Mr. Charles Burnham noticed an account of the Highgate inquest in the *News of the World*, and forwarded it through Mr. Redhead to the Aylesbury police. Mr. Joseph Crossley had also seen some report of it, and he sent it to the C.I.D. with a cutting reporting the Blackpool inquest. The Aylesbury police communicated with the Blackpool police and with headquarters, which then, through Detective-Inspector Neil and Inspector Cole and P.S. Page, commenced elaborate investigations in over forty towns in England, taking statements from 150 witnesses, of whom 112 were called at the trial, and examining the details of one account at Parr's Bank, Herne Bay, of accounts at three branches of the London City and Midland Bank, at Tunbridge Wells, Bath, and Portsmouth; of accounts at the Capital and Counties Bank at Bristol, Cheltenham, and Weston-super-Mare; of one account of the National Provincial Bank at Weston-super-Mare; of another of the Wilts and Dorset Bank; and of two of the London and South-Western Bank at Highgate and Shepherd's Bush, to say nothing of six Savings Bank accounts, of which four were in the names of Smith's victims and the other two in the names of John Lloyd and George Smith.

The police communications between Highgate, Blackpool, Aylesbury, Bath, Bristol, and to the C.I.D. have been placed at my disposal by Mr. Neil. As they are documents of a confidential nature, I have so handled them, quoting here and there to make a point that does not appear in the evidence. It seems that Mr. Schroder was not satisfied about the Highgate death, and would have preferred an open verdict. Mr. Kilvington, for the Lofty family, was, however, satisfied. Mr. Burnham had always suspected foul play, but felt he could do nothing in the face of the Blackpool verdict. The astute Mr. Neil, even as late as January 19, 1915, went so far as to write, "Although we have no real grounds for suspicion that the death was otherwise than accidental . . . it is desirable that he should not have the money in question for a while." Great precautions were used to prevent Smith suspecting that he was under observation, and that inquiries were being pursued about him.

The police did not receive information from Herne Bay until Mr. Lloyd was already charged with the two later murders. It was on February 15, 1915, that Inspector Neil told the prisoner that he had reason to believe he was identical with Mr. Williams, whose wife had died in her bath at Herne Bay. On the 19th of that month her body was exhumed, examined by Dr. Spilsbury, and reinterred. In his report of February 20 the Inspector adds, "I am of opinion that we have not, so far, discovered the full list of this man's crimes."

A feature of the proceedings at the Police Court was the inordinate interest taken by women in the accused; they would, as early as eight o'clock in the morning, take up their station in queues outside the Court, bringing lunch with them, and they literally hemmed the prisoner in, by pressing so closely around the dock that they actually touched him.

The verdict at the inquest was the subject of Parliamentary inquiry, and on July 14, 1915, Mr. Raffan asked the Home Secretary whether he would institute an inquiry into the circumstances which led to the verdict of accidental death being returned at the Coroner's inquests on the bodies of Bessie Mundy, Alice Burnham, and Margaret Lofty, whose deaths were subsequently shown to have been caused by murder, and whether he can state the legal and medical qualifications of the Coroner who held the inquests. Sir John Simon, "I will look into this matter, but its consideration must stand over until the Court of Criminal Appeal has dealt with the prisoner's appeal against his conviction which is now pending"; and on July 22 Mr. Booth asked an identical question. Sir John Simon merely referred him to his previous answer.

The trial at the Central Criminal Court opened on June 22, 1915, and lasted until July 1. It was the longest and the most important murder case tried in England since Palmer's, sixty years before; in one respect it constituted a record—no fewer than 264 exhibits were put in; the witnesses came from over forty different towns, and numbered 112, of whom 18 were solicitors, or solicitors' clerks, and 14 were officials from banks.

The legal and medico-legal aspects of the trial receive special consideration in the next section; the full report of the story cannot be given here, but the entire eight days of its consideration abounded with dramatic incidents. To the horror of Mrs. Millgate, when she saw the naked corpse behind the door, and the amazement of Miss Rapley at Mr. Williams's appalling callousness, may be added the dramatic incidents, when Mrs. Crossley, of Blackpool, and Miss Blatch, of Highgate, were taken by counsel over the very moments when, unknown to them at the time, the murderer was at his dreadful work in the little bathrooms above where they were sitting in the peaceful pursuit of household duties.

Not even a verbatim report can convey their emotional distress, but I will quote a few words from the official report kindly lent by Sir Edward Marshall Hall.

MR. BODKIN: Whilst you and your daughter and son-in-law were in the kitchen, did you notice anything about the kitchen?

MRS. CROSSLEY: I noticed the ceiling.

MR. BODKIN: What did you notice about the ceiling?

MRS. CROSSLEY: The water was coming through.

MR. BODKIN: Would you like a little water?

MRS. CROSSLEY: No, it worries me to think of the time.

．　　．　　．　　．　　．　　．　　．　　．

MR. MARSHALL HALL: Did you think he had something to do with his wife's death? Now then, answer me the question. (The witness mumbled something.) I cannot hear a syllable.

MR. JUSTICE SCRUTTON: Ask the question again! Somebody moved or coughed just at the time we wanted to hear.

MRS. CROSSLEY: I shall not answer the question, what I thought.

MR. HALL: You won't answer the question?

MRS. CROSSLEY: No.

MR. HALL: If you won't answer it——

MRS. CROSSLEY: I cannot answer it, what I think about that.

But she had already answered what she thought about it, by what she wrote on the back of exhibit 175. The postcard on which Smith had left his address, "Wife died in bath, we shall see him again!"

Miss Blatch, after that terribly grim story of the splashing heard above, the wet arms on the side of the bath, and the final sigh, the organ pealing forth its funeral notes for full ten minutes from the sitting-room, the slamming of the front door, the ring at the bell, the calling out to the dead woman, was asked, "Where were you when he so called out?" "At the bottom of the stairs." "Did you go up then?" "I said, 'I cannot come, Mr. Lloyd.'"

"I rushed upstairs to another gentleman I thought was in the house . . . I rushed to the door. I did not notice anything. . . . He said he would go for the police. I said I would go myself. . . ."

MR. JUSTICE SCRUTTON: Did you put on your hat before you went out?

MISS BLATCH: I put no hat on.

MR. JUSTICE SCRUTTON: When you saw the prisoner with
the body in his arms and the legs in the bath, did you look
for any time?

MISS BLATCH: No, I looked for no time; I felt her arms
and went downstairs.

The defence was, as in Palmer's case, the least impressive
part of the trial. Never, except in the Sandhills crime,[1] was
Mr. Marshall Hall so destitute of material; his miserable
client—all the bravado knocked out of him, and speaking,
when he interrupted to his own detriment, in a voice which
a lady present likened to a patient's when only partly under
chloroform—was an impossible witness, damning though
his absence from the box necessarily was. Counsel com-
bated the theories of Drs. Spilsbury and Willcox, and
employed a favourite argument with him, namely, that one
would have to go back to the days of the Borgias to find
such depths of wickedness as the prosecution alleged. One
substantial point he made—Would Smith, if he had intended
to murder Miss Burnham or Miss Lofty, have gone to the
expense of an endowment policy, when for about half the
premium he could have got an all-life policy, which would
have served his purpose just as well? As will be seen,
Smith only abandoned the all-life policy on Miss Burnham
when a further premium was demanded from him to cover
the risk of marriage; and he probably found that an endowment policy masked his designs better from his two brides,
besides furnishing his advocate with a plausible argument. Still, it must have cost Mr. Smith a pang to forgo
£500!

The inevitable verdict was reached on the final day in a
very few minutes. Some reporters, who must have been

[1] The murder by Holt, between Blackpool and St. Anne's, of
Mrs. Elsie Breaks, who had just made a will in his favour,
bequeathing him the amount of her life policy. It well illustrates
"the desperate and short-sighted wickedness" of murderers that
Holt committed his murder within four miles of the similar murder
by Smith, by whose fate he was unwarned.

poorly accommodated, said that the prisoner heard it unmoved; in truth he collapsed, so that a doctor stood near
him. He was "very pale—almost livid. That tell-tale patch
of red on his high cheekbones flushed angrily." Called
upon by the Clerk of Court, his lips refused their office.
"Then, with an effort, he gasped, 'I can only say I am not
guilty.'"

Like Baron Bramwell in sentencing the *Flowery Land*
pirates a half-century before, the judge forbore to add anything to the words of his sentence, but, unlike the Baron,
he concluded with the usual invocation of heaven to be
merciful to the doomed man's soul. It is no part of a
judges' statutory or other duty to add these words. Smith
thanked his counsel, the judge thanked the jury, and
Inspector Neil, and thus ended one of the most remarkable
murder trials, both from the atrocities of the criminal and
the ingenuity with which the net was spread around him by
the C.I.D., in the annals of British crime.

Smith was removed to Pentonville, pending his appeal,
which was heard on July 29. A violent thunderstorm raged
during the proceedings, and, after a peculiarly loud peal of
thunder, the accused man looked nervously at the roof of
the Court, as if he seemed to read his destiny in the wrath
of the heavens. Mr. Marshall Hall traversed much the same
ground in his main argument as at the Old Bailey—that
there was no *prima facie* case of the murder of Bessie
Mundy apart from evidence of system; that such evidence
was not admissible until a case to go to a jury had been
built up *aliunde*. If the prisoner had given evidence that
the death was accidental, then such evidence of system was
admissible in rebuttal, but was not admissible in chief;
there was no evidence of any physical fact by the prisoner
causing Bessie Mundy's death, and no evidence as to surrounding circumstances ought to have been given in respect
of the deaths at Blackpool and Highgate; that evidence of
what took place at Mr. Annesley's was improperly admitted,
as it was an interview between solicitor and client, and

therefore there was a privilege not to disclose it; that the question put to both Dr. Spilsbury and Dr. Willcox, was the death consistent with accident? was *the* question for the jury, that the suggestions of the judge that the prisoner might have lifted the bride into the bath and that he might have employed drugs were improper, as supported by no evidence; and that Mrs. Thornhill's twice-repeated remark about the prisoner's sentence of two years had improperly influenced the jury. Mr. Bodkin shortly replied on the circumstantial evidence of an act of murder followed by evidence to show design, and he commented on the position of the body as inconsistent with epilepsy, which was very unlikely to begin at thirty-five years of age. Mr. Hall did not reply. The Court, after the Lord Chief Justice had paid a compliment to the powerful and able argument of counsel —none the less forcible for being condensed so as to deal with the real points of the case—dismissed the appeal. The prisoner, who had only once taken his gaze from the faces of his judges, turned ghastly white, and was at once removed.

He remained at Pentonville until August 4, when, pursuant to his sentence under Palmer's Act, he was removed to Maidstone. The few remaining days of his life he passed in great prostration and almost constant tears. On August 9 he wrote a letter to Edith Pegler. He listened to the Wesleyan minister who was sent to comfort him and to the chaplain; but he discovered no trace of penitence, and made no confession. His execution was fixed for August 13, at eight o'clock, Pierpont and Ellis being the executioners. The last morning found him in a painful state of collapse; he was assisted to the scaffold, which it took three minutes to reach—thrice the usual time—from the moment the executioners entered the condemned cell. Outside a large crowd had collected, many of whom were women—and many women of all ranks gazed from the windows of neighbouring houses—and the loud babble of their voices could be heard in the cell while the preparations were being made, and the voice of the chaplain was drowned as he recited the opening words of the burial service. As eight o'clock struck a great silence fell on the multitude, and it lasted while the helpless man was almost carried in a blaze of summer sunshine across the prison yard to the fatal shed. He had to be supported on the drop.

What were his thoughts? It is idle to speculate. Had he ever heard of Nero and his cunning and cruel attempt to drown his mother Agrippina? Had he, with his smattering of book knowledge, ever heard of the last recorded utterance of the most infamous of the Imperial Caesars— *Qualis artifex pereo*? If, stupefied and terrified as he was, he was incapable of coherent reflection, we may be sure his last thought was one of self-pity—what an artist to perish, to have thought out a new mode of murder, and only to end like any common cut-purse of the old hanging days!

At the inquest held the same day in the prison, evidence was given that death was instantaneous and painless from fracture of the cervical vertebræ; the body was formally identified by Inspector Neil, and then consigned to the destroying quicklime—naked as his brides had lain naked —exposed to the gaze of strangers.

> *Deep down below a prison yard*
> *Naked for greater shame,*
> *He lies, with fetters on each foot,*
> *Wrapt in a sheet of flame.*

II

The principles regulating the admission of evidence of as at the trial turned on the principle of A. G. *v.* Makin, as to which the lay reader may stand in need of some enlightenment.

The main contention raised in points of law in the appeal other acts than that charged, in order to show system, are discussed in a number of authorities, and are somewhat too technical for a full analysis intended mainly for the general public.

When such evidence is admitted, it is admitted to show, "not that the defendant did the acts which form the basis of the charge, but that, if he did such acts, he did them intentionally and not accidentally, or inadvertently, or innocently." Only a minority of the cases illustrating the principle were murder cases. Palmer's case is often put forward by legal purists as a case where, though there were other indictments against the prisoner for the murder of his wife and brother, the suggestion of the murder of these "was never made or hinted at." A broad distinction between a case like Palmer's, on the one hand, and Smith's or Armstrong's, on the other, is that in Palmer's case the defence was that Cook's death was due to natural causes, and not to misadventure or suicide. That other persons Palmer had access to had died mysteriously was, therefore, regarded professionally as a matter of prejudice. Of well-known murder cases, in which such evidence was admitted, R. v. Geering was a charge of the poisoning by arsenic of the prisoner's husband in September, 1848; there were three other indictments against the prisoner charging her with the murder of her son, George, in December, 1848; with the murder of her son James, in March, 1849; and with the attempted murder of her son, Benjamin, in the following month, all by the administration of arsenic. The evidence of the circumstances of the later death and of the illness in the last case was admitted by Lord Chief Baron Pollock on two grounds (1) to show that the death of the husband, whether felonious or not, was occasioned by arsenic; and (2) to enable the jury to determine whether the taking of the arsenic was accidental or not. It was not admissible as tending to prove a subsequent felony.

Neill Cream's case was another of murder by arsenic poisoning. It was a very celebrated trial, but it did not figure in the law reports, nor did Mr. Justice Hawkins give any reason for admitting the evidence, because, as he stated in a letter to Mr. Justice Windeyer, any comments he might have made in pointing out the relevancy of the evidence would have been very prejudicial to the prisoner. The murder of which Cream was convicted was of an unfortunate named Matilda Clover, and, the defence suggesting in cross-examination death from delirium tremens, evidence was given, after the close of the direct evidence relating to Clover, of the death of three other unfortunates with the same symptoms, and of the attempted administration of a pill to a fourth, who, however, evaded taking it. In the letter referred to Mr. Justice Hawkins goes, I think, rather further than any British authority has gone, when speaking judicially. "I dissent," he wrote, "from the suggestion that such evidence . . . can only be admitted in corroboration of a *prima facie* case which a judge would be justified in leaving to a jury if it stood alone. The admissibility of evidence in itself material and relevant to the inquiry can never be dependent on whether it is used to corroborate evidence already given, or is offered as an independent piece of evidence."

The principle has been well stated in R. *v*. Francis (false pretences) by Lord Chief Justice Coleridge—"It seems clear . . . that when the fact of the prisoner having done the thing he is charged with is proved and the only remaining question is, whether at the time he did it he had guilty knowledge of the quality of his act or acted under a mistake, evidence of the class received must be admissible. It tends to show that he was pursuing a course of similar acts, and thereby raises a presumption that he was not acting under a mistake."

This was applied in the New Zealand case of R. *v*. Hall, where the prisoner was tried for the murder by antimony of Henry Cain on January 29, 1886. The hypothesis of accidental administration was distinctly before the jury. The judge, wrongly as it was held, admitted evidence to show that from June to August 15 of that year the prisoner was in attendance on his wife, and that antimony was found in his possession and in her excreta. In holding the evidence improperly admitted, the Court said—"The evidence is admissible as proof of the intent, where the prior fact of administration has been sufficiently established by independent testimony . . . by prior proof must be understood that there was sufficient evidence of the fact to go to a jury. This preliminary question the presiding judge must determine."

In the case before them the New Zealand Court of Appeal saw no satisfactory evidence of a design, which required for its achievement the deaths of Cain and Mrs. Hall—in other words, there was no *nexus* between the two deaths.

A. G. *v.* Makin is now generally regarded as the leading case, and the instructive judgments of the New South Wales Court of Crown Cases Reserved are quite as valuable as the report of the case in the Privy Council. Its resemblance to Smith's case lies in the presumption of the physical fact constituting the murder charged from the evidence as to the other deaths; in other words, of the facts showing system. Just as Smith was never proved to have been in the bathroom at Herne Bay when Bessie Mundy was expiring there, so the Makins were never proved to have done any physical act to Horace Amber Murray by which he could have been deprived of life. The homicidal act—its manner unknown—was inferred from the facts showing system, the other bodies found, and the overwhelming evidence of motive. The state of the law will be found clearly summarized in Mr. Herman Cohen's edition of Roscoe's *Criminal Evidence*.

The law appears as a result of the authorities to be this:

1. No direct rule can be laid down as to the moment at which evidence of facts showing system becomes admissible. Roughly, the moment is when its relevance appears clear to the presiding judge.

2. Direct evidence of the physical act constituting the crime is not necessary before evidence of system becomes admissible.

3. The introduction of such evidence, tending to prejudice the accused, is not permissible before an issue has been raised in substance, if not in words, to which it is relevant, e.g. in Smith's case, that he was absent from the bathroom at all material times.

4. The evidence, to be admissible, must be (a) to prove a course of conduct; or (b) to rebut a defence of accident or mistake; or (c) to prove knowledge by the prisoner of some fact.

5. Whether such evidence would be admissible if there were no *prima facie* case without it, *quære*.

This was the matter left in doubt in Smith's case; as the Court expressly said, "We have come to the conclusion that there was . . . *prima facie* evidence that the appellant committed the act charged quite apart from the other cases." Mr. Justice Windeyer had said in the Makins' case, "it appears to me that the evidence . . . need not amount to such a case as would be required to justify the judge in leaving it to a jury."

Mr. Marshall Hall's contention that the judge should not have put to Drs. Spilsbury and Willcox the question whether the deaths could be consistent with accident, as that was *the* question for the jury, recalls a conversation between Lord Brougham and Lyndhurst in old age; they were discussing Sir Francis Buller's oft-criticized question—whether the laurel water, in his opinion, was the cause of Broughton's death—to the great Hunter in Donellan's case. Lyndhurst—"I think that Buller had no right to put the question. The point was not in the province of any witness—it was the very question which was to go to the jury. What do you say, Brougham?" Brougham—"Buller was wrong; there can be no doubt of it whatever."

III

All cases of death from asphyxiation, whether proceeding from drowning, hanging, strangulation, or suffocation, present certain characteristic post-mortem appearances. Shakespeare has given an enumeration of them in language of which all men have long recognized the beauty, while medical men have recognized its fidelity.

Warwick, gazing on the corpse of Gloucester in the second part of King Henry VI, Act III, Sc. II, exclaims:

> See how the blood is settled in his face.
> Oft have I seen a timely parted ghost,
> Of ashy semblance, meagre, pale and bloodless
> Being all descended to the labouring heart,
> Who in the conflict that it holds with death,
> Attracts the same for aidance 'gainst the enemy;
> Which with the heart there cools the ne'er returneth
> To blush and beautify the cheek again,
> But see, his face is black and full of blood,
> His eyeballs further out than when he lived,
> Staring full ghastly like a strangled man;
> His hair uprear'd, his nostrils stretched with struggling,
> His hands abroad display'd, as one that grasp'd
> And tugged for life and was by strength subdued.
> Look on the sheets, his hair, you see, is sticking;
> His well-proportioned beard made rough and rugged,
> Like to the summer's corn by tempest lodged.
> It cannot be that he was murder'd here,
> The least of all these signs were probable.

Where, however, a death is due to drowning—and many bodies die in the water from other causes, such as syncope, shock, or a stroke—only about 25 per cent., according to Ferrier, die of pure asphyxia, while in 12·5 per cent. of deaths in the water there is no asphyxia at all. Suspension of efforts at respiration due to early loss of consciousness effect the post-mortem appearances, both internal and ex-

ternal. Less water is swallowed; there is congestion of
blood in the face, and less bloody froth in the lungs and
mouth.

Death may occur from drowning without any water being
found in the stomach. As to the time sufficient to produce
death, where there is complete submersion, if the efforts to
breathe are continuous—in other words, if consciousness is
not lost from some independent cause—one minute and a
half will suffice. In one case there was complete insensibility
within a minute. Where a girl fell into the water in a state
of syncope, she recovered after six minutes' immersion; and
trained divers, who, of course, do not attempt to breathe
under the water can remain submerged for two or more
minutes, but of two divers going under water with apparatus
whose air supply was cut off, one who was brought to the
surface within a minute and a half survived, while the other,
who was not brought to the surface under two minutes,
did not survive.

As to the degree of violence necessary to overcome the
resistance of an adult who is being murdered in this manner,
Taylor says in the *Dublin Quarterly Journal of Medical
Science*, 1853: "It is the result of twenty years' experience
of these cases that the resistance which a healthy and vigorous person can offer to the assault of a murderer intent
upon drowning . . . her, is in general such as to lead to
the infliction of a greater amount of violence than is necessary to ensure the death of the victim." Apart from the
mysterious blood in the Mundy case, there was no evidence
of violence in any of the three cases, except slight bruising
of an arm in the Lofty case.

But this authority, high as it is, needs to be profoundly
modified where the struggles of the victim are confined by
the sides of a bath. There being no example of a similar
murder to those alleged against Smith to be found in any
works on forensic medicine, one of the detectives engaged
on the case persuaded a young lady of his acquaintance,
who was a practised swimmer, to sit in a bath, in a swim-

ming costume, which was filled to the same height as the Herne Bay bath. She was aware that the experimenter was about to submerge her if he could; she was aware that his intentions were not felonious, and she was accustomed to having her head under water; yet with all these circumstances in her favour as compared with Smith's victims, she was unable to get her head above water, after it was once submerged, and consequently unable to cry out, and she almost instantaneously ceased to struggle, whereupon the experiment was at once discontinued; but not before the experimenter had satisfied himself not merely of the possibility, but of the ease, with which an ordinarily vigorous man could destroy life in the manner in which Drs. Spilsbury and Willcox opined Smith might have murdered Miss Mundy.

Other experiments carried out in empty baths satisfied several detectives that, using certain means, a woman might be held under water without inflicting any bruises upon her.

I will now proceed to a separate consideration of the three cases. The Herne Bay bath was five feet long, inside, at the top; three feet eight inches along the flat bottom; the width at the sloping end was two feet at the top and one foot six inches at the bottom; at the other end it was one foot seven inches and one foot one and a half inches. Its depth was one foot four inches at the sloping end, and a quarter-inch more at the other end. The deceased was five feet nine inches high, and this was the position in which Dr. French found her—"The face was upwards, the trunk at the sloping end, the feet out of the water resting on the side of the bath a little below the edge. The position of the body kept the legs from slipping down. The head was submerged and the trunk partially so. The mouth was under water; her arms rested by her side. The right hand contained a piece of soap. The bath was just over three-parts full. (In other words there was at least twelve inches of water in the bath.) The legs were out straight—straight from the trunk."

As to the theory of epilepsy, which was accepted by the jury, I will let Dr. French speak for himself—"Further than his saying that she had temporarily lost consciousness, he could not get anything very definite out of him." Although the grounds for regarding it as an epileptic fit were very slight, he prescribed bromide of potassium (not only a specific in epilepsy but a general sedative). The probability of a woman having her first epileptic fit at thirty-five appears to be over twelve to one. Quain stated that only six per cent. of cases first occur after thirty years of age. The probability of a person having a fit of this sort and not giving the warning scream, which is so characteristic as once heard never to be forgotten, is about three to one.

The probability of a person having such a fit and getting into the position described, the lay as well as the medical reader can judge for himself.

Mr. Mowll and his jury did not see the bath nor ascertain the position of the body in it; they had no measurements, and they never tested, as Inspector Neil did, the possibility of the bath being filled by the deceased woman in the half-hour that Smith said he was out of the house.

The theory of epilepsy finds little support, again, from the post-mortem appearances; the face was dusky—blue all over—and much congested with blood; there was froth, which flowed out of the mouth, and on pressing the chest water flowed out of the mouth, facts indicating continued efforts at respiration after the face was submerged, and negativing the notion of a fit.

The piece of soap clutched in the right hand was a matter of some comment. Counsel spoke of the expression that "drowning men clutch at a straw" as figurative. In a sense it is; but the figure of speech rests on a well-known truth of forensic medicine. There is unusual unanimity amongst the authorities on this point. Professor Glaister refers to "the presence of objects in the firmly clenched hand—as weeds, grass, sticks, or other objects," as a safe indication that death was due to drowning.

"It is certain," says Poore, "that a man who is drowning does clutch at anything with which his hands come in contact." "The presence of substances clutched in the fingers —due, in the first instance, to a vital act subsequently rendered permanent by instantaneous cadaveric rigidity—is evidence of submersion during life" (Dixon Mann). "Vain clutchings are made at whatsoever comes within reach. The indications of such instinctive efforts form the most important evidence of submersion during life" (Ferrier). It is also generally stated by the authorities that instant *rigor mortis*, lasting until putrefaction, is more common in drowning than in any other form of violent death met with in civil life.

Re-examined as to the soap, Dr. French said that if a person died suddenly with a piece of soap in her hand the grasp would be continued after death; and Dr. Spilsbury, recalled, said, "If only consciousness is lost, the soap would probably drop out of the hand by the relaxation, but if death occurred immediately, then the object might be retained owing to his condition of instantaneous death stiffening," and the body would retain its ante-mortem position. Taylor has stated that some of the bodies after the Regent's Park disaster of 1867 were "stiffened in the attitude of active exertion, the hands and arms being thrown forward as if sliding or skating." In that case, however, the cold may have produced stiffening by solidification of subcutaneous fat, which may have been confounded with true *rigor mortis*.

A difficulty that remains as to the piece of soap is that if Dr. French's memory was to be trusted after three years, cadaveric rigidity had not set in when he saw the soap in the hand. "I do not think it was stiff. . . . It was limp." "Any part of it was not stiff?" "No."[1]

[1] The firm clutching in the hand after death of articles retained by it *in articulo mortis* is common to all cases of asphyxia. Mary Patterson, Burke and Hare's beautiful victim, had twopence halfpenny, which she held fast in her hand. Mrs. Hostler, another victim, had ninepence halfpenny in her hand, which they could

A word as to the blood seen by Mrs. Millgate about the waist of the body. As Mr. Marshall Hall seems to have suggested that each fatal seizure occurred during a period —a suggestion that renders Smith's conduct in each case still more astounding and revolting—it may, with diffidence, be suggested that this blood, the nature of which was never explained, may have been due to post-mortem bleeding from the vagina. In the case of the "Ireland's eye" murder, Mrs. Kirwan was found to be bleeding from the ears and private parts. After the conviction of Kirwan, Dr. Alfred Taylor contributed a paper and Dr. Thomas Geoghegan another on the medico-legal aspects of the case. Dr. Taylor wrote: "It is a rare condition of asphyxia and not a constant accompaniment or sign of the suffocation or strangulation of females." And he adds, "I have not known it to occur in drowning." Dr. Geoghegan, from the experience of colleagues, found it quite common in the strangulation of women in judicial and suicidal hanging. "Vaginal bleeding has been frequently noticed in hanging and strangulation," he says, but while admitting that the "subject appears not to have sufficiently attracted the attention of medical jurists," he seems to regard it as peculiar to death from strangulation, as apart from other forms of asphyxia.

It will probably suggest itself to medical readers that the great venous congestion in all cases of asphyxia may render such post-mortem bleeding no less likely in asphyxia from drowning as from other causes of death of the like sort. In the few cases in our reported criminal trials there were other things to account for the bleeding that was observed, and authority is very scanty in the treatises on legal medicine.

The *cutis anserina*, which Dr. Spilsbury found, was of little importance in determining the cause of death. It is a sign of exposure to water at the time of death, and not of

scarcely get out of it after she was dead, so firmly was it grasped.— Burke's *Courant* Confession, Appendix I, *Trial of Burke and Hare* —Notable British Trials Series.

death from the immersion in water. Dr. Spilsbury agreed
that it was found in sudden deaths, other than from drowning, but the weight of authority seems to be that *cutis
anserina* has no value bearing as on the cause of a death
occurring in water.

A last word on the Mundy case. Smith, it will have been
noted, informed the relatives that "Bessie died of a fit in a
bath." That is not what Dr. French said—he was always
clear that death was due to drowning—but the appearances
in the case of a body of a man of thirty who died of an
epileptic seizure in a bath and not from drowning have
been recorded by Taylor. Much congestion of the brain
was noted, in the right ventricle only a small clot of blood,
otherwise the cavities of the heart were quite empty. The
body of Miss Mundy was so decomposed when Dr. Spilsbury examined it that he could say little as to either heart
or brain.

In the case of Alice Burnham, very little water was
found in the body by Dr. Billing—so little that he even
doubted that death was due to drowning. As we have seen,
the absence of water is not inconsistent with death from
drowning. The Blackpool bath measured five feet three
inches long; the width at the sloping end was two feet three
inches at the top and one foot two inches at the bottom;
at the tap end the width was one foot three and a half
inches, and one foot at the top, and the bottom respectively.
The depth at the centre was eighteen inches; and the bath
was full to within one and a half inches of the top, even
after the head was raised out of the water. The body was
quite limp when Dr. Billing saw it; he opined that death
was due to drowning, but we are without any description
of the post-mortem appearances in this case. From the
absence of anything about the colour of the face or of a
bloody froth about the mouth and lungs, and from the small
quantity of water found, it is a legitimate inference that
death in this case was not brought about solely by asphyxiation, but that there may have been an early loss of con-

sciousness before the efforts to breathe had become very
distressing.

As to the theory of epilepsy in this case—and it was
hardly maintained by Mr. Marshall Hall—not only was
there no suggestion of the monitory scream, but a history
of an alleged fit at nine years of age, followed by no more
at the critical period of puberty, and only succeeded by one
after a will just made in favour of an impecunious husband
about seventeen years later, may justly be dismissed as of
no importance, as Dr. Bertram Stone dismissed it, "because
the history is so indefinite."

The post-mortem appearances in Margaret Lofty's case
point to asphyxiation as the main cause of death. The lips
were blue and swollen, the whole of the face was congested
and the eyelids swollen, and there was froth exuding from
the mouth and nostrils. Of violence the only traces were
one externally visible bruise above the left elbow on the
outer side, and other bruises, recent, beneath the surface.
Dr. Bates perceived no blood near or about the body; some
bloodstains on an undergarment were susceptible of a very
obvious explanation, and indicated neither violence nor the
existence of a period at the time of death. Evidence of old
pleurisy and peritonitis was noticed by Dr. Bates, but no
suggestion was made that either disease had any bearing on
the death. There was no evidence as to the position of this
body in the bath. When first seen after the murder by Miss
Blatch the corpse was being held up by Smith over the bath,
the legs being still in the bath, and whether she had faced
the sloping or the narrow end was not made clear. The
bath was five feet six inches long at the top, four feet two
inches along the flat bottom; at the top of the sloping end
it was two feet one and a half inches, narrowing down to
one foot six inches. At the tap end the width was one foot
six inches, narrowing down to eleven and a half inches.
There was no evidence as to the height of the water in the
bath.

A view remains to be examined, which may serve to

explain the extraordinary sexual familiarity which established itself so early and so easily in the relations of Smith
with his brides—the last in particular. It was brought to
my notice by a correspondent that hypnotic suggestion
might have played a part in causing these three women, not
only to place themselves in the very singular situations in
which they did, but even, without physical effort on the
part of Smith, to drown themselves! Sir Edward Marshall
Hall, whom his conspicuous and my more modest public
engagements prevented my conferring with until a late stage
in the preparation of this essay, in a letter states: "I am
convinced he (Smith) was a hypnotist. Once accept this
theory, and the whole thing—including the unbolted doors
—is to my mind satisfactorily explained." Little is known
to professors of legal medicine in England of the power of
hypnotic suggestion to cause a person to do an act morally
or otherwise repugnant to him or her.

Arbert Moll, as quoted by Georges du Bor, states that
hypnotic suggestion plays no part in the seduction by a man
of a woman. That woman would have given herself to that
man anyhow. A. E. Davis, Professor of Psycho-therapy to
Liverpool Hospital, in his *Hypnotism*, after ridiculing the
sexual psychology of *Trilby*, in which Svengali, by mesmeric
art, compels the surrender of the heroine to his revolting
person, she being all the while in love with little Billie,
proceeds to state that, in his experience, it is quite impossible, by hypnotic suggeston, to compel persons to do an
act which is morally, æsthetically, or on grounds of religious
or similar scruple repugnant to them.

Such, too, was the effect of the evidence of Dr. K——,
now a member of the Bar, in a case in which he was plain-
tiff in a contested probate action, and in which he was
alleged to have induced his lady patient to make a will in
his favour. His defence succeeded. On the other hand, the
authorities collected by Wingfield in his *Introduction to the
Study of Hypnotism*, are far more guarded. Moll thinks
that, by repeated hypnotic suggestions a person could be

"willed" to commit a crime. Forel proved this by compelling a subject to fire twice at a man with a pistol, loaded, but not to his knowledge, with blank cartridge. Von Eulenberg, von Schrenck-Notzing, and other eminent German and Austrian psycho-therapists seem to agree. I think I am correct in stating that in Russia once, and in France twice, a woman has successfully put forward as a defence in homicide hypnotic compulsion by a man. Lord Justice Scrutton informs me that he accepts neither the hypnotic theory nor the theory that poisonous vapour was put in the bath water. Digital pressure *per rectum* on the spinal column is an alternative based on a doctor's personal experience with a violent lunatic.

In my view the simple explanation that the unhappy women were in love with Smith explains all. The respondent, in one of the two famous political divorces of the mid-eighties, said of the co-respondent, "If Charles had asked me to stand on my head in the middle of Piccadilly, I would have done it."

Certain definite evidence, moreover, indicates the use of some physical violence by Smith, the hair at the sloping end of the Blackpool bath, the overflowing of water from it, the sound of the wet arms and the sighing, as of one struggling to get breath, at Highgate. Smith's own autograph note to Mr. Shearman, which that learned counsel gave to me, to my mind, went strongly to show that he—an ex-gymnasium instructor—knew how to accomplish such murders without bruising the victim. And the experiments of Mr. Neil confirm the possibility.

IV

A popular and prolific French author (M. Paul Bourget) has in a work marked by all the vigour of youth and all the enthusiasm for his subject of a good Frenchman, endeavoured to analyse the constituents of a "lady's man." Looks count for little. Education for nothing. "Mais le

tact de l'homme à femmes est quelque chose de tout par-
ticulier—presque un organe—comme les antennes chez les
insectes—presque un instinct, car l'éducation n'y ajoute
guère. Cet homme, par exemple, du premier coup d'œil,
juge exactement quel degré de chance il a auprès d'une
femme à laquelle il est presenté. Il dira mentalement—
Celle-ci est pour moi, celle-là, non." And after a consideration of typical men he concludes, "Mais ils avaient tous ce
fond de tempérament où gît la force vitale."

Smith's protective antennæ seem to have guided him well
enough in the search for likely victims; where they failed
him was in the inability to warn him of the women in whom
his pronounced sexuality aroused an instant and an enduring antagonism. On men, on the other hand, he produced
no impression, but one of insignificance and commonness—
"Just like any butcher," was Mr. Neil's appreciation.

It has long been recognized that two radically different
types of men favourably impress women; the type possess-
ing a marked femininity of character enabling its possessor
to understand women from their own point of view, and
those of a very pronounced masculinity, who succeed by
riding rough-shod over the finer feelings of women, and
whose success is due to the arousing of woman's primitive
desire to be mastered—a desire which is normal within
limits, but when abnormal is styled by the professors of
sexual psychology masochism, to distinguish it from its
counterpart, the abnormal desire to inflict pain (within
limits psychological in the male at least), which is known
as sadism, each term being derived from the man of letters
who stands as a type of the abnormally submissive, and
the abnormally masterful and cruel.

George Joseph Smith was undoubtedly a male whose love
for mastery over women, including the infliction on them
of humiliation (witness the letter to Bessie Mundy of
September 13, 1910, the circumstances of each desertion
of a robbed bride, and the invariable exposure of the nude
corpse of a murdered bride to the gaze of strangers of

either sex) approached the pathological limit where the normal masculine desire merges into sadism; but, unlike Neill Cream, Chapman or Jack the Ripper, Smith was not driven to murder through an overmastering impulse of sadism, the pecuniary motive being the all-powerful one, murder being only undertaken where robbery could not be accomplished without it. In Cream's case the motive of pecuniary advantage through blackmail was very unsubstantial, and there is little doubt that the half-crazy doctor was a victim of the most dangerous of sexual perversions, one which accounts for a great deal of what is most unsavoury in the divorce court. As to the physical attractions of Smith, he had, it seems, a certain magnetism about his eyes. A woman writer in a popular morning paper has told of the "irresistible feline luminosity in the eyes," of the sexually attractive man; and Smith's first bigamously married bride has described him thus—"He had an extraordinary power over women. This power lay in his eyes. When he looked at you for a minute or two you had the feeling that you were being magnetized. They were little eyes that seemed to rob you of your will." He was accustomed to indulge in such practices as wife-beating. "Often," says the authority quoted, "he has beaten me black and blue. Once he locked me in a cabinet folding-bed."

Smith made no pretence of fidelity to this bride; indeed, the occasion of one flogging arose out of an amour. I will give the story in the woman's own words. "Often he used to brag to me about his numerous women acquaintances. Once I met one of his victims with him and warned her to her face about him. She was greatly shocked, and said she had always regarded him as a good, religious man. That night he came home and thrashed me till I was nearly dead." Whether or not his various "victims" were so simple as to believe in his whole-hearted devotion, it remains an everlasting truth that women are not much attracted by want of enterprise in the male. To a wife, at least, to have a roué for a husband is an indirect compliment to herself. As Valera says, "Even the most moral and religious young woman likes to marry a man who has loved many women; it gives a greater value to his choice of her." Professor Hans Gross well says, "Only the very young, pure, and inexperienced girl feels an instinctive revulsion from the real roué, but other women, according to Rochebrune, love a man in proportion to the number of other women who love or have loved him. This is difficult to understand; but it is a fact that a man has an easy task with women if he has the reputation of being a great hand with them. Perhaps this is only an expression of the conceit and envy of women, who cannot bear the idea that a man is interested in so many others and not in themselves. As Balzac says, 'Women prefer most to win a man who already belongs to another.' The inconceivable ease with which certain types of men seduce women, and at whose heads women throw themselves in spite of the fact that these men have no praiseworthy qualities whatever, can only be so explained. Perhaps it is true, as is sometimes said, that here is a case of sexuality expressing itself in an inexplicable manner." Johnson's famous dictum falls naturally alongside the Austrian jurist's. "'Ladies set no value on the moral character of men who pay their addresses to them; the greatest profligate will be as well received as the man of greatest virtue, and this by a woman who says her prayers three times a day.' Our ladies endeavour to defend their sex from this charge, but he roared them down: 'No, no; a lady will take Jonathan Wild as readily as St. Austin, if he has threepence more. . . . Women have a perpetual envy of our vices; they are less vicious than we, not from choice, but because we restrict them.'"

Havelock Ellis has observed that, "There is no such instinctive demand on woman's part for innocence in a man," but he adds by way of qualification, "This is not always or altogether true of the experienced woman."[1]

[1] *Studies in the Psychology of Sex*, vi, 44.

But while, as we have seen, Smith without money,
manners, education or even appearance to recommend him,
produced invariably an effect on women, though that effect
was at times the reverse of favourable, men carried away
no distinct impression of him. Mr. Burnham did, indeed,
dislike him, but so faint was the personal impression that
he was unable to pick him out at Bow Street. One witness
alone, Mr. J. R. Robbins, is shocked by Smith's greed after
money—when he claims half-commission on the murdered
Blackpool bride's policy; but for the most part the quiet
professional men, with whom he comes in contact, see
nothing to notice about him. The solicitors, the doctors,
the bankers, house-agents, insurance agents—even the
coroners, those men of more than ordinary perspicacity—
to each and all he appears in no wise out of the ordinary; indeed, upon the bank managers he must have
produced a mildly favourable impression, for he opens
account after account in false names, without references,
and in one case to the manager's knowledge has only an
accommodation address, "where they call themselves con-
fectioners. It is a sort of small mixture of milk and
groceries." P.C. Heath, who, as having had a good opportunity to notice him at Bismarck Road, was asked by
Inspector Neil to keep watch for him outside Mr. Davies's
office, was unable to identify him. His eyes with their
suggestion of mesmeric powers apart, there was nothing in
his appearance or manner that struck Mr. Shearman, who
had constant opportunities for studying him at Bow Street
and at the Central Criminal Court. His main endeavour
seemed to Mr. Shearman to be to pass for a gentleman of
independent means and of culture. To produce such an
impression, he went so far as to wear a frock-coat and tall
hat at Herne Bay in August, where such raiment would
certainly arouse remark.

Yet he had only to be in physical propinquity to a
woman, and she at once became aware that she was in the
presence of a man of some mysterious powers over her sex.

To the wife of a high legal functionary he appeared an attractive man; that acute criminologist, the late H. B. Irving, during the trial was seated next two fashionably attired ladies of pleasure, and these vied with one another in praise of the prisoner's charms. At the police court the eagerness with which women thronged round him in the dock was the subject of indignant comment in the papers; and at the Old Bailey the police had special instructions to make it as difficult as possible for women to be present. On the other hand, even in cold print, the dislike of the man that instantly possessed such witnesses as Mrs. Tuckett and Miss Rapley appears unmistakably.

There is one masculine failing which women find it peculiarly difficult to overlook in a man; yet Smith possessed this failing in a marked degree—petty meanness in the matter of money. To Edith Pegler he sends only the smallest sums, and his ideas of a honeymoon jaunt stop short at places which are either free to the public or are to be entered for a modest expenditure; it is Brockwell Park, the National Gallery or a shillingsworth of the White City; and he leaves Alice Reavil to pay for the food!

"In all the transactions of his infamous life," wrote Mr. Sims in *Bluebeard of the Bath*, "whether he was Jekyll or whether he was Hyde, he was abominably mean. He never squandered a farthing of his ill-gotten gains. He rarely, when absent from his Bristol wife, sent her any money. When he decided to murder Miss Mundy he bargained for the bath, did not pay for it and when he had committed in it the murder for which he had obtained it, he sent it back again, not even paying a small amount for the hire of it, although by using it he had obtained between two and three thousand pounds. He never wasted a farthing on any of the young women whose money he was going to get by murdering them. When arrested, although he had made many thousand pounds by the most economical form of murder possible, he was wearing a suit of clothes for which he had not paid. They had not been paid for when he was hanged."

He sells Bessie Mundy's clothing before it has come back from the laundry and does not settle the laundry bill, which Mrs. Millgate has paid. He disposes of Alice Burnham's wardrobe and rings, and grudges her remains a pitch-pine coffin when deal would do as well. He takes Miss Mundy away from Weston-super-Mare, and does not settle with Mrs. Tuckett the £2 10s. owing. He takes Mr. Crabbe, a working man, away from his work to witness his marriage and does not pay him a penny. He promises to remunerate Mrs. Crossley for her trouble, and gives her nothing but his address for her to forward him the local papers. And he tries to get out of paying Mr. Annesley's bill.

Though he claims half-commission from Mr. Pleasance over Alice Burnham's policy, he leaves her mother and brother to pay for their modest lunch at the "Company House" where he has choked the life out of their dear one. But when he is in danger himself, no considerations of expense restrain him from securing what he deems the best professional aid.

How it came about that such a man was able to impose his will so absolutely on three different women, each coming from a home superior to his, and each boasting a greater degree of education, and to leave on each an impression of kindness, truthfulness and genuineness so absolute that, forsaking the natural ties of the flesh, they surrendered all, to them, that they had in the world—their bodies and their belongings with equal abandon—can best be treated in a study of the criminal himself in some detail.

v

The fascination which very depraved men exercise over women has long stimulated criminologists to discover— hitherto with little success—what common attribute bad men possess which makes them so ingratiating to the sex.

"Duval, the ladies' pride, Duval, the ladies' joy," in common with the other highwaymen, doubtless owed his success to the false romanticism with which the *Beggar's Opera* and less enduring literary tributes contrived to invest the lives of the knights of the road. But the uncomely Sheppard, the hideous Peace, the commonplace Palmer, those "two singularly common and ordinary persons," Pranzini and Prado, and many another whose crimes are unsung, were equally, in their day, the objects of passionate adoration, in some cases on the part of women much above them in station, and their shameful and well-deserved ends a fruitful cause of tears and heartaches.

"This former conductor of Pullman cars," observed M. Bourget of Pranzini, "is mourned in many a lady's bed." Smith, however, like Dougal, the Moat Farm murderer, belongs specifically to that small band of criminals, of whom Vitalis is an exemplar, who thrived on the exploitation of feminine weakness, and, so far as is known, avoided forms of crime in which the ability to deceive women would not have availed.

The resemblances between Dougal and Smith are more than superficial. The Moat Farm murderer had also been in the army, and his known relationships with women included (1) Miss Griffiths, whom he married, and who died in Canada under suspicious circumstances, being hastily buried without a death certificate: (2) a second wife, a young woman of means whom he married on August 14, 1885. She died in a few weeks in Halifax, Nova Scotia, and was buried beside the first wife in a neglected grave; (3) a Halifax girl, with whom he lived and by whom he had a child. He several times threatened to murder her, and abandoned her; (4) a widow, by whom he had two children, and whom he then left to take small positions in clubs at Stroud Green and Southend; (5) a young unmarried woman of means, with whom he got in touch through a matrimonial agency. He induced her to live with him and to sell her property and give him the proceeds; (6) the third Mrs. Dougal, a good-looking woman, whom he married against her parents' wishes in August, 1892; (7) an elderly lady, with money, who took a public-house for him at Ware. He was suspected of arson here, and was convicted of forgery; (8) his last victim, Miss Camille Holland, an elderly lady of means, whom he met after serving his sentence. She was very musical, artistic, and literary, and also very religious: in point of education and status she was far above Dougal. Yet she lived with him as his wife without scruple.

At the time of the murder of Miss Holland, Dougal was endeavouring to seduce—if that word be not too mild to cover what went to the verge of an attempted crime—their maid, and he was industriously running after several other young women in comparatively humble life. In all cases the women's property was at his disposal equally with their persons. He had the education of an N.C.O. of the old-time Army, but was far from being a man of polish. Educationally, however, he was the superior of Smith. "Mr. Philip Curtin" and others, having represented Smith as a man who affected *belles-lettres* and who could turn out a pretty sonnet or *billet-doux* to a lady, let me here say, once and for all, that a man with smaller pretensions to literary skill one could not come across. He was utterly incapable of writing a grammatical sentence or of spelling the commonest words. In a note before me now he writes "wader" repeatedly for "warder," and "difficulty," "voilence," and "brusies" for the familiar words they are meant to represent. In a letter to the secretary of a West End club he writes, "dissadvantage," "attatched," "obivious," and "conserned"; and in a letter to Mr. Davies he writes "in fain," "attemt," and "solomn." Like some better educated people, he never could distinguish "principal" from "principle." Though we had been at war with Germany for nearly a year when he was tried, the acquaintance of Mr. Smith with public affairs and with history was well evinced by the note in which he speaks of "several jerman or foreign women." As for his grammar it was nearly as bad as his heart, and sufficiently appears from his letters put in as exhibits.

What, then, is the explanation of the fascination of Dougal and of Smith? Readers of Havelock Ellis will remember that that shrewd observer has remarked that nowhere does the trained observer meet with more sensual women than are to be found in quiet homes and country vicarages. What to the common eye seems a demure young woman of the middle-class is to the eye of *le vrai homme à femmes* a woman who may worship at the chapel or in her father's church, but in secret she is also a worshipper of the pagan divinity Priapus. "Those cunning little eyes," which "blinked uneasily" while Mr. Justice Scrutton was lashing their possessor with his tongue, could read very well the mind of a woman, and could see whether in the depth of her eyes could be traced the smouldering fires of passion, all the more ready to burst into flame from the constant repression of desire forced on her by the daily round and common task, be it governess or lady's companion or young lady in business.

And having once gained the sexual mastery, how absolute is the villain's control! He writes to Bessie Mundy—"I have caught from you the bad disorder; for you to be in such a state proves you could not have kept yourself morally clean." He decamps with Bessie's money, and apparently with most of her clothes, and when they next meet, at Weston-super-Mare, "there he was looking over the sea," and despite the remonstrances of Mrs. Tuckett, she goes off with him in her shift, not troubling to come back to pack a bag with a nightdress! He takes her to the solicitors, and there, before her, concocts the most unblushing lies—it is he who, through some indiscretion, had supposed himself infected. The man of law writes as instructed. Smith writes to the brother in stilted style reminiscent of poor Aram's compositions—"I know not how I shall offend in dedicating my unpolished lines to you, nor how you will censure me for using so strong a prop to support so grave a burden"—and Bessie adds, "My dear Howard I trust you will try and forget the past as I have done"—(she who had written, "The man came across my path. . . . I am very sorry. . . . I feel it is a mercy I am rid of him. I do hope my husband will be caught. I feel I have disgraced myself for life")—"I know my husband now better than ever before. You will be pleased to know I am perfectly happy." Perfectly well, according to Dr. French when he last saw her alive about 3 p.m. on Friday, she sits down to write that letter, which arrived with the telegram announcing her death. "I have made out my will and left all to my husband." What art has the monster practised that deep-rooted loathing and deserved contempt are banished and confiding submission rules this poor creature on whom Death is so soon to lay his icy grasp?

Alice Burnham, though younger in years than either of the other murdered brides, was more accustomed to the ways of men. She had contracted a malady, which was not named in Court, though it was discussed in the evidence of Dr. Bertram Stone, under re-examinaton, and again in the cross-examination of Dr. Spilsbury when recalled. It had set up septic peritonitis, and, without lifting the veil, which the Court suffered to remain drawn, it may be added that it was thus alluded to in a letter from Dr. Stone to the North British & Mercantile Insurance Company, "I have obtained leave both from Mrs. George Smith and her husband to give full details of the unfortunate episode in her life. Mr. George Smith is aware of all that occurred."

The knowledge so obtained by Smith may account in a measure for the influence wielded by him over the least weak-willed of the victims. How absolute that influence was appears from the correspondence. Alice writes to her father on November 22, giving him until the first post on November 25 to pay her the £100; but on the 24th of that month she had already instructed solicitors "to take extreme measures." It has taken only some two months for

Smith to root out all her natural affection and sense of filial
duty, and to plant in their stead a boundless belief in
himself—"I have the best husband in the world," wrote
the deluded, doomed bride, a few short hours before she
was robbed of life.

If, in reviewing the ghastly sequence of events during the
few days at Blackpool, one may permit oneself to indulge
in the whimsical method of De Quincey and to recognize
that, "murders have their little differences in their shades
of merits, as well as statues, pictures, oratorios, cameos,
intaglios, or what not," then the murderer will be seen to
have advanced in his dreadful art since the Herne Bay
affair. So certain is he of accomplishing his object that he
carries out the crime in a room directly over one he knows
to be in occupation; having fulfilled it, he descends to that
room, and, struggling to appear unconcerned, engages in
talk about a fire engine! He must have learned something,
too, about the possibility of resuscitating the apparently
drowned; alone, at 80 High Street, he can leave his victim
submerged for as long as he pleases, but in the Company
House every moment is precious. The murderer returns
with his bride just before eight; about 8.15 the water is
observed to be dripping through the ceiling; at 8.35 Joseph
Crossley is summoned back from his work to fetch the
doctor to what Smith knows to be a corpse. Immediately
Dr. Billing sees Alice Burnham he exclaims, "She is dead."

Tidy has recorded a case, which must surely be exceptional, of recovery after twenty minutes' immersion. Smith
on each occasion was present when artificial respiration
was tried. It would need the pen of De Quincey or Edgar
Allan Poe to conjure up the scene, if at Regent Road,
Blackpool, or Bismarck Road, Highgate, Smith had watched
the return of animation and had beheld the awful physical
traces of his crime one by one disappear under the doctor's
art—the congested blood leave the cheeks, the lips resume
their normal hue, the eyes, "staring full ghastly," take on
again the tender look they wore when conscious life was

suspended, and then, as comprehension came back, had seen the "bride" lift her accusing finger, from which he had already snatched the rings, fond emblems as she supposed of hallowed love, to denounce the cold-blooded assassin, who but a few short hours before had held her in his arms and caressed her with all the tenderness with which devotion can mask the impetuous desires of the lover!

When we dwell on the commonplace incidents—the fatal Friday, the tapioca pudding, the inquiry if it had been relished, the evening stroll, the appalling deed while the homely north-country family are enjoying their late tea below, the casual entry of the murderer—"full of agitation" withal—and realize that every detail of this seemingly insignificant winter's day was part of a well-laid scheme thought out many weeks before, and that the sinewy arms, while they hold the bride in the transports of love are cunningly measuring her powers of resistance to a very different description of attack, we realize how utterly apart from normal men, even from criminal men of other types, the cold-blooded mercenary murderer stands. One would have thought that Nature would have stamped on the lineaments of such fiends some warning of their dreadful characters; yet it has not been found so. De Quincey says of Williams: "The concurrent testimony of many witnesses, and also the silent testimony of facts showed that the oiliness and snaky insinuation of his demeanour counteracted the repulsiveness of his ghastly face, and amongst inexperienced young women won for him a very favourable reception."

A correspondent of mine whose father had once travelled with Palmer in a railway carriage, tells me that the father was very favourably impressed by the all-persuasive *bonhomie* of the poisoner. Hideous as Peace was, he was yet ingratiating. Nature seems to have endowed murderers with an extraordinary plausibility; they have a popular facility in lying, which Sir James Stephen noted a generation ago.

Nemo repente venit turpissimus, sang the Roman satirist,

and Smith, in his last crime, was destined to transcend even his own performances. From the time Margaret Lofty left Bath (after those untruthful missives to her relations about the mythical old lady) to the time when P.C. Heath was summoned to her dead body at Bismarck Road, was but some thirty hours. The bridegroom, his dreadful purpose locked in his bosom, comes at three in the afternoon of December 17, to the house in Orchard Row, and is repulsed from the door. There was "a bath that a person might lie in," in that house, and the man fears he will be baulked of his prey. His rage finds free vent in the street. He drags off his feverish bride to other apartments, then to the doctor's, where she is naturally silent. Next day—and by what endearments he charmed away the vexations and anxieties of that Thursday and smiled away her maiden shame, murder all the while in his heart, my pen shall not essay to set forth in words, our language has no vocabulary in which to record such infamy as man never yet had descended to—next day, any suspicion Margaret might have entertained has vanished. It is nothing to her that he has been afraid to meet her relations; that he has compelled her not only to conceal the approaching marriage, but to lie about it, and to lie to the insurance company. It is nothing to her that at the cheap apartment-house, where he has booked rooms for the honeymoon at 16s. a week, a detective in plain clothes has refused him admittance. Overnight she has written from the second lodging-house, where she was so soon to meet her death: "He was a thorough Christian man, whom I have known since June. He has been *honourable* and kept his *word* to me in everything. . . . I am perfectly happy."

In the whole rogues' gallery there surely was never a knave so plausible as this, never one who, until detection came and his self-control suddenly gave way, could so completely mask his feelings.

Any man who reads carefully as to what happened at Bismarck Road, about which, as the learned judge observed,

it is difficult to comment, must be aghast at the psychological puzzle this amazing criminal presents. The passionate lover of a single day's wedded life, just a week after
the murder, sits down and pens the very bald and business-
like statement. It reads: "Certificate of birth, certificate of
marriage, certificate of death, wife's will, policy, receipt
for premium paid, official acceptance, receipt for burial."

One recalls that page in Palmer's diary, where under the
date 21st, Wednesday, is recorded, ". . . Cook died at ten
o'clock this morning. Jere and William Saunders dined.
Sent Bright a 3 mos. Bill," and under the date 25th,
Sunday—25 after Trin. "At Church Hamilton preached—
dined Yard."

And yet superior persons wonder why, since bad people
do not take any interest in the lives of good people, good
people perversely wish to read about bad people!

But what elevates Smith to the highest pinnacle of infamy
is that he played upon the very tenderest and most sacred
of all our feelings to accomplish his crimes. Of bigamists
and seducers and betrayers of women there have been and
will continue to be many notable examples; but, complex
as our human nature is, Smith provided the first, as his
judge believed he would also furnish the last, instance of
a man caressing in his closest embraces of marital love a
woman, the exact moment and manner of whose death at
his hands he had in his mind, while his lying lips were
uttering to her words of the purest passion. He is wholly
apart, from the point of view of sexual psychology, from
the lust-murderer or mutilator, whose sexual erethism dis-
charges itself in the commission of an act of homicide, or
maiming, or in some form of infliction of pain. Smith plays
with every success the part of an uxorious and devoted
husband, and all the time the exact cash value of his bride
to him as a corpse is present in his mind. The tender words
and sighs of passion, fondly believed to be reciprocated, are
breathed into ears which will hear unmoved in a few hours'
time those same lips sighing and panting for life as the

cruel water closes over them and for ever puts them to silence.

It would need more than De Quincey's pen, even, to call up before the shuddering reader that scene in the bathroom at Bismarck Road. The poor bride, her whole being throbbing, with a temperature of 101, the tiring winter's afternoon in which there has been so much to do, a will to make here, money to withdraw there, closed by the fall of night, returns to their modest rooms; at once he soothes her; Miss Blatch enters, and there she is on her knees by the fire and he reading the paper—a picture of domesticity! She would like a warm bath; there are reasons; she would feel more comfortable. Utterly confiding, the bride of a day lets her bridegroom come in and invade her privacy. The natural shame of a woman before a man is gone already. She has given herself to this honourable Christian man, and thenceforth she is his.

It is not decent to speculate—save in the privacy of the individual mind—as to what exactly happened in those few fatal moments round about eight o'clock on the night of December 18. It is barely possible to hold the pen and in the mind's eye try to visualize the scene.

The muscular arms, that could rend a chair asunder, are wrapped around the yielding body, his eyes look into her eyes, the melting, liquid light of passion shining in each. A last tender kiss seals eternally those words of love. The strong hands grip the unresisting body; a fierce, feline look steals into the cunning eyes that a moment ago beamed so kindly. As her head plunges under the water what thoughts flood the mind of Margaret Lofty? Drowning people, we are told, in the brief space of consciousness left them, pass in review every incident of their lives. What recollections and reflections must have raced through her brain! Each caress, every tender word, those letters, in which were revealed the harmony of their souls—all rushed back to her in that crowded last moment of consciousness. And he?

He is looking with professional concern for the signs,

which are the heralds of death. The eyeballs are beginning to project—good! The face is blackening—excellent!
She did get her head above water for a second and gave
a little sigh; that was disconcerting, but it will pass for
nothing, and he has locked the door. All will be over before
he unlocks it. He can lift her head out of the water now,
and judge the progress of the case. A bloody froth streams
from mouth and nostrils—it is finished! Now to steal to
the parlour downstairs and play as unconcernedly as he
can upon the organ. What notes did it peal forth? Some
dirge? Some *marche funèbre*? Then out into the bleak
night on an errand to buy tomatoes. And when he comes
back there is that knocking on the door which, as in *Mac-
beth*, transfers our sympathy ("of comprehension by which
we enter into his feelings and are made to understand them
—not a sympathy of pity or approbation") to the murderer.
"In the murdered person all strife of thought, all flux and
reflux of passion and of purpose, are crushed by one overwhelming panic. The fear of instant death smites him with
its 'petrific maze.' But in the murderer . . . there must be
raging some great storm of passion, jealousy, ambition,
vengeance, hatred—which will create a hell within him; and
into this hell we are to look." Thus wrote De Quincey in
Murder Considered as One of the Fine Arts.

Smith, not being "such a murderer as poet will con-
descend to," the hell within him provided no material for
sublime tragedy; merely materials for one of the longest
and costliest murder trials these islands have ever known.

And if we could look into that hell within him, after he
heard the fatal words, "this appeal is dismissed," the only
torments we should find him suffering from would be
"chagrin at the mistake in not securing immunity." The
mercenary murderer, without exception, can find no con-
trition. The learned judge in passing sentence must have
realized this. "An exhortation to repentance would be
wasted on you." And in the two last letters from Maidstone, the one to his solicitor, the other to Edith Pegler,

the usual canting and hypocritical expressions are mingled with the usual invectives against his judges and the unjust world which has consigned an innocent man to his doom.

The history of crime, like other history, "With all her volumes vast, hath but one tale." His end was like the end of all others, except that he met it abjectly.

"The world contains," wrote Sir James Stephen, "an appreciable number of wretches who ought to be exterminated without mercy when an opportunity occurs."

Though

> *Fate will use a running noose*
> *For the best man and the worst,*

I do not think the most ardent advocate of the abolition of capital punishment will deny that fate, through the instrumentality of Messrs. Pierpont and Ellis, made a most proper use of her running noose on August 13, 1915.

RONALD TRUE

(1922)

By Donald Carswell

I

RONALD TRUE was born in Manchester in 1891. His parents
were very young, his mother being a mere child of sixteen
—a fact which becomes significant in the light of his
mental history. The circumstances of his birth seem to
have been unfortunate, but his nurture was in no way
prejudiced. He was well cared for from birth; and when
he was about eleven years old his mother made an exceed-
ingly advantageous marriage, and was thenceforth enabled
to make a provision for him that was not only adequate,
but generous. He had every provision that affection, backed
with money, could afford. His childhood was healthy and
remarkably free from illness, and he grew up into a
powerfully built young man, well above the average height.
Sound bodies, however, do not necessarily contain sound
minds. Even in early childhood True's conduct was peculiar
and disquieting. That a boy of five or six years should tell
lies, play truant, and be cruel to his pets is in itself no
great matter. Such incidents often constitute a phase, ugly
but transient, in the childhood of perfectly normal indivi-
duals. They may indeed be interpreted as no more than the
first crude attempts of the self-conscious being to assert
himself against the world. The normal individual, having a
capacity for social education, is quick to recognize their
futility, and the ugly phase passes. But where the phase
does not pass—but develops and deepens—where the lying
becomes extravagant, the truancy persistent, the cruelty
insensate—there is a presumption of congenital defect

170

which at the crucial periods of adolescent and adult life, will manifest itself in clearly defined neurosis and even insanity.

So it proved with Ronald True. When he was entering his teens, his aunt, Mrs. Angus, who had not seen him for several years, found that the abnormality he had evinced at the age of six had noticeably increased. Her evidence on the point is couched in very general terms, but there is no reason to doubt its veracity. One may quite well have a clear impression of a person's character and yet be able to give few illustrations or particulars. Demeanour, as every lawyer knows, is eloquent to him who observes it, but what it tells is well-nigh incommunicable, particularly after the lapse of many years. One curious incident, however, remained engraved in Mrs. Angus's memory. True's mother fell seriously ill, and Mrs. Angus informed the boy of the fact. He was not at all distressed, but merely remarked, "Oh, well, if she dies all her property will be mine, and I'll give you her two best rings straight away, and you can have anything you like of her things and jewellery." This remark was made, apparently without any consciousness of impropriety, by a boy of fourteen, who, as far as can be judged, had always been on affectionate terms with his mother.

True was at this time at Bedford Grammar School, where he remained until he was nearly eighteen. Although it does not appear that he was guilty of any outrageous conduct, his reports were consistently bad, and indicated incapacity for sustained mental effort. In the circumstances it is not surprising that his family made no attempt to put him into a profession, but took the conventional way of disposing of a stupid youth. They shipped him off to the Colonies. It was thought that farming in New Zealand might suit him, so to New Zealand he went. Within a year he was back in England. New arrangements had to be made. A Yorkshire farmer was induced to take him as a pupil. That lasted a month. The Yorkshire farmer could do nothing with him. The next move, in 1911, was to the Argentine. In 1912 he was again on his mother's hands in England. Then Canada was tried. He served in the North-West Mounted Police, but not for long. Subsequently he seems to have drifted to Mexico, but not much is known of his movements until the middle of 1914, when he turned up in Shanghai. He was there when the outbreak of the war in Europe gave him the best of pretexts to return home once more.

Let us pause here. To the casual glance True's career up to this point suggests no more than a born wastrel with possibly some indications of mental defect. But, while no detailed information is available as to his behaviour between 1909 and 1914, three facts were ascertained that are full of significance to the alienist, viz., that during the critical years of adolescence (eighteen to twenty), he was leading a vagabond life, incapable of acquiring any settled mode of livelihood; that during the same period (as will appear) he had acquired the morphia habit; and that on his return to England the peculiarities of his demeanour had noticeably increased.

In the early years of the war, when recruiting methods were still very imperfect, it was inevitable that many unsuitable persons should have been accepted for service. But even when all allowances have been made, it is hard to understand how this weak-minded narcomaniac should have had no difficulty in joining (of all branches of the service) the Royal Flying Corps, and getting a nomination to a flying school with a view to a commission. Of course, he would never have been accepted had his drug addiction been known. That his own family should have been unaware of his habit is, perhaps, not very surprising, but it is curious that the medical men who passed True should have had no suspicions. In due course True became a cadet at Gosport Flying School. His career there was not encouraging. He failed repeatedly in the simplest examinations, and how in the end he managed to pass no one who knew him then has ever been able to imagine. In the air he was not only reckless but incompetent, and during a cross-country trial flight he crashed badly at Farnborough. A month later he had another but less serious accident at Gosport, escaping with a few cuts and bruises. The Farnborough crash, however, was undoubtedly a bad one. No bones were broken, but he suffered concussion of the brain, from which he lay unconscious for two days. It is said that subsequently True had at least two more accidents—one at Yeovil and one in America. If he did have an accident at Yeovil, which is doubtful, it was not a serious one. On the other hand, he did have *one* bad crash in America. True's own statements about his flying mishaps were extremely confused and inconsistent.

From the time of the Farnborough crash, True's malady developed rapidly. His abnormality had always been notorious in Gosport; but after the Farnborough accident, according to the testimony of former cadets, he was regarded as little removed from a madman. His general demeanour is described as feverish, nervous and imbecile. On being awarded his wings, he appeared at mess wearing a pair that he had had specially made of extraordinary design and three times larger than regulation size. He could hardly ever be induced to wear his cap, alleging (probably the truth) that it hurt his head. To meet the requirements of ·military discipline he went about with his hat in his hand, putting it on, only for saluting purposes, whenever a superior officer appeared.

The Gosport accident in March, 1916, may be said to mark the end of True's military career. Shortly afterwards he was invalided out of the Air Force. As the official medical records are not available, the precise circumstances of his discharge cannot be stated. All we know is that, in a Southsea theatre one night, shortly after the crash, he had a sudden and violent seizure of pain in the right hip. Of their charity True's family spoke of the attack as a result of his accident, but all the indications point to a syphilitic condition. The Wassermann test showed a negative result, but True's own statement was that he had suffered from syphilis. Syphilis is admitted to be a prolific cause of mental derangement; but it is doubtful if it had much bearing on True's case. The medical witnesses called in his defence obviously did not attach much importance to it. He was taken into the Alexandra Military Hospital at Cosham, where, by his refractory and often offensive conduct, he made himself such a nuisance that there was general relief among the staff when his mother managed to arrange for his transference to a private nursing-home at Southsea. It was at this time that his drug addiction was discovered. The pain in his hip was so severe that morphia had to be prescribed. The ordinary dose had no effect whatever. The patient would not respond except to doses that proved his long experience of the drug. Naturally, what he got by prescription was quite insufficient for his craving, which he endeavoured to satisfy by all sorts of surreptitious methods—bribing orderlies and cajoling chemists in the town. Generally, his moods alternated between childish exaltation—as when he went about in a bath-chair with a hooter and a doll—and depression with sudden fits of violence. In addition, the chauffeur, Sims, who is the principal authority of True's behaviour, during this period, states that he had frequent and serious lapses of memory and occasional terrors of a delusive nature such as that an assassin was lurking at the back of the theatre box.

After this, which brings us down to the end of 1916, it is distinctly surprising to find a Southsea lunatic turning up in Yeovil early in 1917 as a test pilot at the Government Control Works! Also it is not surprising to hear that the works officials found him utterly unsuitable for the job. He had lost nerve badly, complained constantly of headaches, was noticeably "moody," and his incompetence as a pilot was manifest and pitiful. He did not stay long at Yeovil, and in June, 1917, we find him in New York, very

much at a loose end, but posing quite successfully as a
war-broken English pilot. It should be said here that, while
everyone who came into regular intimate contact with True
regarded him as a lunatic, in casual social interest he was
capable of creating an excellent impression. His manner
was plausible and even engaging. He was, according to
some standards, very good company. And in the circumstances of the moment he had no difficulty in being taken
at his own valuation. The United States had just entered
the war, and no one was disposed to inquire into the antecedents of an invalided English Flying Officer, who spoke
with assurance (albeit without a vestige of truth) of his
service in France, his honourable wounds and the German
airmen who had met their doom at his hands.

Among those who heard True's fairy-tales was a young
actress, named Frances Roberts, who was so deeply impressed that before the year was out she married him. She
never suspected that her hero had never been to France,
that he was unfit to be trusted with an aeroplane, and that
his discharge from the Air Force, so far from being due
to "honourable" wounds, was caused by injuries brought
about by his own incompetence, aggravated by morphia.
It was a foolish and disastrous marriage, but one can hardly
blame Mrs. True when we consider that the same year
True was able to persuade the United States War Department that he was a suitable person to be employed as an
instructor in their flying school at Mineola. When the
school was transferred to Houston, Texas, True went with
it. His wife, having to fill a theatrical engagement, did not
accompany him, and did not see him again until June, 1918,
when he returned to New York in poor health. His history
during the intervening months may be stated quite briefly.
His employment at Houston, as might be expected, came to
a speedy end. He thereupon wandered down to Mexico,
where he developed a chest complaint that kept him in
hospital for a considerable time. From Mexico he crossed
over to Cuba, and thence returned to New York, once more

at a loose end. The usual thing happened. Within a month
he was back in England with his mother, and this time the
prodigal had added to the problems of his return by bringing a young wife with him.

True's mental condition was now serious enough to
justify drastic measures. The evidence of Mr. Morgan, a
flying officer, leaves no doubt on the point. Mr. Morgan
had known True at Gosport in 1916, and regarded him as
deranged then. He did not see him again until shortly after
the Armistice, when he met him in London several times,
and found that he was in a distinctly worse condition, and
not accountable for his actions at all. But True's family
took no action, and that is not surprising. Nothing is more
difficult than to try to get a lunatic's relatives to admit he
is a lunatic. Often nothing short of the dire realization that
the wretch's neck is in danger will make them face the ugly
fact; for, bad as it is to have a near relative in a lunatic
asylum, it is worse to have had one hanged. But at the end
of 1918 there was nothing to suggest that True would be
dangerous to anyone but himself, and so, instead of con-
sulting a medical specialist, his family were once more
trying to find him suitable employment, at a comfortable
distance from England. As usual, a job was found. In
February, 1919, accompanied by his wife (who was shortly
expecting a baby) he sailed for the Gold Coast, to take up
an appointment with the Taquah Mining Company. Within
a few weeks of starting his duties as assistant manager in
the native compound he was under suspension. From the
moment of his arrival his conduct had been intolerable.
His extravagances of talk and behaviour made him the
laughing-stock of the station, and even natives summed him
up as "the massa what live with him mammy (wife) and is
sick by him head." There could only be one outcome—
dismissal; and so True was packed off home, having been
on the Gold Coast less than six months. The ostensible
reason for his discharge was that the climate did not suit
him. The real reason was that the company had no time for

a notorious drug-addict who hobnobbed familiarly with the blacks, and behaved like an imbecile Munchausen among his fellow whites. But True does not seem to have been at all downcast by the circumstances of his departure. He assured the people of Taquah that they would soon see him again, as he intended to form a transport company for the Gold Coast trade. His return to the Gold Coast would be by aeroplane, *via* France, the Mediterranean, and the Sahara! When it was objected that this was a bad route for petrol supplies, True did not agree. There were many places, he said, where oil and petrol could be had, but he omitted to give particulars.

Taquah was the last job True ever had. His family seem to have realized the futility of trying to put him to work. It was less troublesome to leave him alone, and make him an allowance sufficient to support his wife and child. Indeed, his condition when he returned from the Gold Coast was such as to put employment of any kind out of the question. Thenceforward, to the time of his arrest, his life was a long dismal history of morphia debauches, punctuated by periodical "cures" in nursing-homes, rapidly increasing mental deterioration, and developments in behaviour that caused his family first anxiety and then genuine alarm. When he returned from West Africa, he was taking morphia in great quantities, and so continued until the beginning of 1920, when his wife and mother decided that something must be done. Accordingly he was persuaded to enter a nursing-home kept by a Dr. Parham at Brighton, where he remained for six months. In the home he was allowed, on an average, about twelve grains of morphia a day. As that was quite inadequate to satisfy his craving he sometimes endeavoured to acquire illicit supplies, and when these were not forthcoming, for the Brighton chemists were soon on their guard against the "madman," as he was called, he was often extremely violent.

Three incidents occurred at this time and are of interest as illustrating a fact of morbid psychology, which, while a

commonplace among alienists, does not occur at all in the
popular conception of the nature of insanity, viz., that
mental disorder is in essence an emotional rather than an
intellectual condition. A man may show little or no intellectual derangement, and yet be as mad as a hatter. Usually,
of course, there is well-marked intellectual derangement,
but it is probably secondary to the emotional disturbance.
For emotion and intellect are far from being self-contained
entities. A good intelligence without the appropriate emotional quality will soon cease to be "good," just as a plant
will languish in improvised soil.

It is not in the intelligence, but in the emotional and
instructive activities of the mind, that springs of conduct
must be sought. (Even the psycho-analysts are agreed with
the alienists on that point.) When one comes to think of it,
the conduct of any creature can mean no more than the
sum of its attempts to adapt itself to its environment, and
in the biological history of such attempts intelligence comes
as a late and probably, at best, an ancillary device. But it
is true of intelligence, as of every *bonus judex*, that its
constant aim is *jurisdictionem ampliare*. Thus men, no
matter how instinctively they may act, always essay to
construct a rational basis for their conduct. This rationalizing takes a more or less comprehensive account of objective
fact, but emotion always keeps it within certain limits.
Regarded as an adaptive function, conduct may be successful or otherwise. In either case the individual will invariably attempt to state a rational basis for it. Thus the self-
made man always feels himself able to explain to the
public "How I succeeded," and the chronic failure is
equally ready—though not with the same eager audience—
to account for his misfortunes. Both cases are eloquent of
the inveterate bias of the ego in favour of itself. The
successful man tends to put to the credit of his own wisdom
matters that are no more than lucky chances. The unsuc-
cessful man is preoccupied with his consistent bad luck.
He is all right, but he has never had a fair chance. In

prosperity the ego must be given a fair chance. That is human nature.

Now when a man becomes insane he does not cease to be human. The forces that underlie his insane conduct are the same in character as when he was sane, but their equilibrium has been destroyed. An emotional disorganization occurs, with consequent failure of adaptation. The intelligence, though it does not as a rule remain unaffected indefinitely, may not decay *pari passu*. It may continue to function fairly well, in which case it will persist in its task of "rationalizing" conduct long after conduct has ceased to be susceptible of rational explanation. If his notions do not accord with the facts, they must be altered as may be necessary. Here we have the initial conditions of a delusion. Presently two more factors come into play—sensory derangement (or hallucinations) and a certain decay of the intelligence that seems inevitably to follow the emotional disorder. The latter need not be extensive. It may never amount to any more than an impairment of the critical activities, which, being the latest development of the human mind, are the first to be attacked; but it is enough. All the conditions are now present for an utterly false reconstruction of the external world, which may proceed to the most fantastic and extravagant lengths. The lunatic thereby reaches a new accommodation, which, however embarrassing to the community, is in a measure satisfactory to himself. The emotional disorder which prevents him from adapting himself to his environment has compensating elements, which enable him to fabricate an environment adapted to himself. These considerations afford a clue to Ronald True's conduct during the period he spent in Dr. Parham's home.

He was not only unemployed but definitely unemployable—a state of affairs not at all in accordance with his own estimates of his deserts. It was unthinkable that so meritorious a person should be without a job, and as no job was forthcoming the obvious solution was to invent one.

Accordingly, he astonished his friends one day by announcing that he had just obtained "a billet, a wonderful billet, with a large salary from the Portuguese Government." Asked for particulars, he produced what he called an "agreement." This was a sheet of paper which bore some puerile nonsense, obviously written by True himself and a penny stamp cancelled by writing in the style of a receipt. On being told his precious agreement was worthless, True broke into tears of vexation and tore it up.

To the same class of conduct belongs the incident or rather series of incidents which we may describe as the delusion of the "other True." While in Dr. Parham's home True occasionally backed horses, and got the racing results by telegram. If the telegram announced a winner, good and well—it was his; but if it announced an "also ran," True was always quite sure it was not for him, but for *another person of the same name*. So with bills. The Ronald True in the nursing-home never owed money, it was always "the other Ronald True." When these facts were given in the trial they pointed to no more than common dishonesty. Such an explanation is inadequate. If the story of "the other Ronald True" was a fraud, it was the fraud of a dement, for no man in his senses could have imagined that anyone would have been deceived by it. Strange to say there was in fact a Ronald *Trew*; but though he came to know of it later there is nothing to show that at the time True knew of his namesake's existence. The point, however, is immaterial. Whether he knew or did not know that there was a person called *Trew*, the device of accepting all agreeable telegrams and referring all the disagreeable ones to a *doppelgänger* was too silly to be regarded as calculated deceit. Psychologically it was of a piece with the bombast which had made him ridiculous in West Africa, and which certainly had not abated when he went to Brighton. His pathological egoism would not allow that he could ever be a loser. His score at golf was always less than the bogey.

He could always give anyone 80 in 100 at billiards. All the horses he backed were winners.

We come now to the third significant incident of the Brighton period. True was wholly dependent on his mother, and had not a penny of his own. Nevertheless he must needs make a "will" by which he purported to leave £100 to Dr. Barnardo's Homes and a like amount to the Battersea Home for Lost Dogs, and directed that his child should be brought up, and indeed adopted, by a lady whom he named. *There was no mention of his wife.* Mrs. True knew nothing of this singular document till some time afterwards, when lighting on it by accident she asked her husband what he meant by it. His reply was in the nature of a repudiation. People did strange things in mad fits and it was unfair of her to tax him with it. On this Mrs. True destroyed the "will," and said no more. The episode is instructive as showing a new phase in True's mental derangement—an incipient hostility towards his wife, for whom, up to this time, he had never shown anything but the utmost affection. Later this hostility became pronounced, and possibly, had not another victim intervened, would have had a bloody consummation.

In September, 1920, True left Dr. Parham's home and went with his wife to Portsmouth, where they lived together for the next twelve months. About the end of the year True informed his wife that he must go to London for a few days to see a Mr. Harris, who, he alleged, had promised him employment. (The name Harris was apt, for there was no such person.) In a few days he was back in Portsmouth but almost immediately returned to London. Not hearing from him for several days, his wife telegraphed to an address he had given her. He replied by letter. "By the time you receive this letter," he wrote, "I shall no longer be in this world. The man Harris has let me down." This was not the first time True had hinted that he might kill himself, but never before had the threat been so explicit. In alarm, Mrs. True hurried up to London, and, after a prolonged

search, ran him to earth in a Soho restaurant—a mental
and physical wreck. His urgent business in London had
been a morphia debauch. His condition being now worse
than ever, he was persuaded to enter a nursing-home in
London for another cure in the spring of 1921, but stayed
there only a week. Probably the home was glad to be rid
of a patient who was not merely troublesome, but extremely
alarming. His violence was such that he had to be looked
after by two male attendants, and the other Ronald True
developed from a fantasy into a homicidal delusion. He
would have to meet the other Ronald True one day, he
declared, and then there would be a "how d'ye do." When
he returned to Portsmouth Mrs. True presently discovered
that her husband had developed a new and very embarrassing habit, viz., pilfering at bookstalls. His thefts were very
petty and quite purposeless. He had no use for the trifles
he stole. It simply was that, when he bought newspapers
or magazines, he must make a point of taking away something—no matter what—more than he paid for. There was
nothing impulsive about these thefts, be it noted; for he
would with great complacency show his booty to his wife
—doubtless to show her what a cunning dog her husband
was. He was never detected. When ultimately he did make
an appearance in Portsmouth Police Court, it was on a
graver charge, namely, obtaining morphia from a druggist
by means of forged prescriptions. He was convicted and
fined.

At this juncture his relatives decided that another attempt
must be made to cure him of the drug habit. An operation
for appendicitis intervened to delay matters, and it was not
until November that he returned to the London nursing-
home for his "cure." As before he had frequent fits of
violence that called for drastic measures of restraint, but
this time his stay was a little longer. He did not leave the
home till the end of a month, when, attended by a nurse,
he went down to Folkestone, where his aunt had undertaken
to look after him and his child during his wife's absence on

a theatrical tour. Mrs. Angus, his aunt, by painful experience was prepared for a great deal, but this time she found her nephew harder to cope with than ever before. Druggists could be warned not to supply him, but as his movements could not be controlled, there was no guarantee that he was not getting morphia clandestinely. His irregular habits and late hours worried his aunt considerably. She remonstrated and got a reply of sinister anticipation. Three palmists, he told her—one in Buenos Aires, one in San Francisco, and one in Shanghai—had predicted that he would be killed through a woman soon, so he meant to have a short life and a gay one. In his general demeanour there had developed a new and ugly quality, which Mrs. Angus tried to describe by saying that his eyes were those of a certified lunatic. His bombast took a repulsive turn. In Mexico, he boasted, he once wrote out his title to a mining claim in the blood of a German whom he had killed for disputing his right.

After the Folkestone visit, which lasted a fortnight, there is a gap of a week or two in True's movements, but he spent Christmas with his mother and his aunt. It was noticed that he was very morose. He spoke little. He took no interest in his child, towards whom he had hitherto been fatuously affectionate. He spent most of his time brooding in obstinate silence over the fire. To Mrs. Angus this gloomy preoccupation was more alarming than any extravagance. She was now convinced that her nephew was not only insane but dangerous, and she and her sister had anxious consultations about what should be done with him. While the discussions were going on True suddenly left home, announcing that he had some business to transact in Bedford. He never returned. His wife, who had just finished her engagement, met him by arrangement in London one day at the end of January. On this occasion he was quite affectionate but not very communicative, and when they parted Mrs. True took it for granted that he was returning to Bedford. The point of fact is that all through this period he never left

London. A week later she met him again. He was no longer
affectionate, but distinctly hostile to her. His conversation
was rambling and incoherent, but she gathered that a Mr.
Davenport had promised him some employment or other,
and that he was going to leave her for good.

From that day until the tragic March 6 True vanished
from his family's ken. The plight of the three women was a
distressing one. They now knew that True was a dangerous
lunatic, and from such stray information as they could
gather, it appeared he was prowling about London with a
loaded revolver in his pocket and murder in his mind. It
was imperative that he should be caught and put under
effective restraint. Mrs. True sought the help of Scotland
Yard, but as no crime had yet been committed Scotland
Yard could only refer her to a competent private detective, and recommended ex-Inspector Stockley. On Friday,
March 3, Mr. Stockley took Mrs. True's instructions to trace
her husband and at once set to work. But it was too late.
On Monday, March 6, True was arrested in a box at the
Hammersmith Palace of Varieties for the murder of Olive
Young, *alias* Gertrude Yates.

II

True, when he was arrested, had been absent from home
nearly two months, during which time, save for two short
meetings with his wife in January and February, he had
held little or no communication with his family. What was
he doing?

His movements during January can only be conjectured.
The only witness who saw him at this time was his wife,
who accepted his story that he was stopping at Bedford on
important business, and had only come up to London for
the day to meet her. This was a pure invention. He had
no business at Bedford, and no prospect of work; and there
is no ground for believing that during all this time he ever
left London, except on crazy "joy-rides," of which more

will be said presently. He was leading a vagrant life about the West End, and no doubt drugging himself heavily. From the beginning of February information about the manner of his life is available in considerable detail. Here is the story disclosed at the trial by the evidence given there.

One evening in the first week in February a Mr. James Armstrong, who among other things had been in the motor trade, but who for the first time was out of work, chanced upon a former business acquaintance in the Corner House, Leicester Square, London. Mr. Armstrong's friend had with him an affable stranger whom he introduced as "Major True." Armstrong and True seem to have taken to each other at once. They arranged to meet again, and the acquaintance ripened rapidly. For the next few weeks they were together nearly every day for hours on end. Armstrong gathered that his friend had been in the Air Force during the war and had done some strenuous service, and that he was now doing civil flying and made several trips to the Continent, often with valuable cargoes. This present employment, he explained, was attended with some risk. There was always the chance of a forced landing in a lonely and dangerous neighbourhood, and therefore he would be glad to buy Mr. Armstrong's automatic pistol, if he was disposed to part with it. Mr. Armstrong was quite agreeable and let him have it with a quantity of cartridges for £2. The two men went about the West End constantly, visiting restaurants and places of amusement. True did most of the paying and, no doubt, according to the notions of an easy-going, pleasure-loving, and undiscriminating man, proved a most agreeable companion. He had a preference for going about hatless. His stories of adventure in distant lands were often uncommonly tall—but that could only be part of his fun, for they were stories that nobody could be expected to believe. Another pleasantry of the "Major's" was that he proposed to form a society of enterprising spirits, who would undertake to "put away" anybody that anybody else found objectionable at the rate of a "bob a nob." Armstrong treated this as a practical joke. It may be doubted if he would have viewed it in that light had he known that after purchasing the automatic pistol and ammunition True's first care was to file the nose of every bullet. There was a further peculiarity of the "Major's" conduct. He was a bit of a vagabond, moving fitfully from one expensive hotel to another, or sleeping in the Savoy Turkish Baths in Jermyn Street. On the other hand his cards bore permanent addresses, a very impressive one in Mayfair. He seemed to have no lack of money and spent it lavishly, and could always command a smart car and a chauffeur. On the whole, Armstrong, who was looking for employment at the time, seemed to have decided that "Major" True was an acquaintance worth cultivating; and he was encouraged in his belief when at a later stage True proposed a partnership in Civil Aviation in the United States. Armstrong was willing, whereupon without more ado True 'phoned to the Cunard Company to arrange for berths and the conveyance of a car and an aeroplane by the next convenient boat. This struck Armstrong as a queer way of doing business, and he began to wonder if his friend were to be taken seriously.

It is worth knowing at this point that all of True's friends (*male*), even those who regarded him as quite mad, saw nothing sinister in his conduct. Even his habit of carrying a loaded revolver in his pocket does not seem to have been taken seriously by men. But with women the case was decidedly different. Among the places of amusement visited by True and Armstrong was Murray's, a well-known dance and supper club. Neither was a member, but on February 5 they went as guests. They were introduced to a Mrs. Wilson, in whom True took immediate interest. At first Mrs. Wilson thought nothing of it, but when he met her at the club she found his attentions rather embarrassing. He forced himself on her to the exclusion of everyone else, and there were things about him that she did not like. Thus in the middle of conversation he would break off, stare about him wildly, utterly at a loss, like one awaking from a dream, until recalled to his surroundings. His attitude of possession towards her became not only offensive but terrifying. Owing to his hip trouble he could not dance with her and forbade her to dance with any other man, declaring that if she disobeyed him "there would be trouble," and enforcing his threat by displaying a revolver which he was careful to point out was loaded with split bullets. In this connexion True told a curious story. There was a man, he said, going about the West End using the name of Ronald True and passing cheques which his (True's) mother had to take up. This man, True suggested, was a dangerous criminal who went about armed, and consequently he, the real True, had obtained permission from Scotland Yard to carry a revolver lest one day he should meet his impersonator. Mrs. Wilson was far from being reassured by this story. She decided that True was a lunatic and must be humoured if he was not to do mischief.

For a week or more she had to endure him. He imposed himself on her as *cavaliere servente*, visiting her at her house, and accompanying her to restaurants and Murray's. The loaded revolver was constantly in evidence, and on several occasions when she hesitated to go out with him she was told that a bullet in the head would be the penalty for a refusal. She dared not say him nay. All she could do was to stipulate that Mr. Armstrong should always be with them. True, she thought, was not a safe man for a woman to be alone with. Apart altogether from his actual menaces, his conversation was disagreeably preoccupied with the theme of murder. He was going to kill the "other Ronald True," or somebody else—it did not seem to matter who the victim was. And of course, in murder, as in everything else, he would be brilliantly successful. "I will murder someone one of these days," he remarked casually to Mrs. Wilson. "You watch the papers and see if I don't. I'm perfectly certain I'll get off. Watch the papers. I want to try it out." Presently the talk of murder passed from the phase of talk into a fantasy.

One day he had promised to telephone Mrs. Wilson at five o'clock—presumably about taking her out in the evening—but no message came. At last, about eleven o'clock, the telephone rang. True was speaking, and he had a horrid tale to tell. He said he had called at his mother's house about six in the evening and, getting no answer, had gone round to the back and entered by a window. All the servants were out, and his mother was lying bleeding on the floor with her head battered in. She was not dead, however, and he had had her removed to a nursing-home. An operation was to be performed next day by a surgeon named *Wilson*, but there was little hope for her recovery. Mrs. Wilson was naturally rather excited, and carefully scanned the papers next day for accounts of the outrage. She found nothing. That evening she met True and asked him how the affair of his mother had not leaked out. His reply was, "I'm keeping it dark, there is to be a big case about it." Mrs. Wilson was puzzled and had inquiries made. She found that the story was a pure invention. What the object of it was she could not divine, but she was confirmed in her belief that True was insane. Suddenly, to Mrs. Wilson's great relief, he ceased to visit her and Murray's and she saw him no more. This was in the third week of February—a fateful week in True's history, as we shall see. It was just about this time, it will be recalled, that True had a meeting with his wife, at which he announced he was going to leave her for good. Thenceforward he eluded all the efforts of his relatives to get in touch with him.

A curious point emerges here. When he first left home, True must have been fairly well supplied with money, but by the middle of February he had spent every penny he had. Yet this was the moment he chose to cut himself off from his only source of income. Probably he suspected a design to have him put under permanent restraint and accordingly was taking no risks. What need to worry about

money so long as he could borrow or steal? He touched
his friend Armstrong for a pound or two. On February 17
the two cronies visited the Ring in Blackfriars Road, where
True seemed to have no difficulty in persuading the referee
to part with £5 in exchange for his I.O.U. That same evening he saw Mrs. Wilson for the last time. Murray's Club
had to be avoided in future. He had cashed a cheque there
that there might be trouble about.

This cheque incident has the interest that it revealed to
True's family what apparently True's family had not realized before, that there was another Ronald True, who,
however, spelt his name Ronald Trew; and Mr. Trew was
a member of Murray's. The two men had never met, but
it is tolerably certain that True knew, and had known for
some time, that he had a namesake. It may have been this
knowledge that started the idea of *doppelgänger* in his
mind. Certainly in his excited fits in the London nursing-
home, he used to complain of the scandal there would be
if a man was going about the streets with a name like his
own. To a disordered mind the fact that another person
bore the same name would soon suggest a sinister purpose,
whence it would be an easy transition to the belief that he
was an enemy, carried a deadly weapon, and so forth.
True's fraud does not justify us in assuming that the story
of the "other Ronald True" was a criminal device and
nothing more. Among the many circumstances that point
to its delusional character is the curious fact that True never
once alluded to it in Armstrong's presence, though he was
free enough about it to other people. For some reason he
seemed to take pains to conceal it from his favourite male
associate, though if he had invented the story simply to
"make evidence," to cover up his misdeeds, this is the very
person to whom the story should have been told. Whether
in passing the cheque at Murray's True forged the name
Trew or used his own name and took advantage of the easy
confusion is not clear. The evidence of the club manager
is contradictory on the point. The fraud, of course, was

soon discovered. Ultimately the club authorities got in touch with Mrs. True, who made good the amount.

True's last meeting with Mrs. Wilson was on February 17. The very next night he found a new victim—the unhappy Gertrude Yates. It is not known when they first became acquainted, but there are grounds for believing that True and Armstrong had once met her casually in some West End lounge and True had taken her address. Gertrude Yates was an ex-shopgirl, twenty-five years of age, who had drifted on to the streets and assumed the professional name of Olive Young. As far as one can judge, she was of the better sort in her calling. She was healthy, temperate and quiet in her habits. She was fairly prosperous, always had money ample for her obligations and had a balance of over £120 in the Post Office Savings Bank. She lived alone in a basement flat in Finborough Road, Fulham, where she was attended by a daily servant.

On the evening of Saturday, February 18, Miss Young had a call from her most intimate friend, a married woman named Dent. While the two girls were talking there was a knock at the door, and presently Olive Young ushered in a tall dark man whom she introduced as "my friend, Major True." Mrs. Dent noticed that Major True had no hat. The newcomer, who was evidently there by appointment, was very polite. If he had only known that Miss Young had a visitor he would have sent her home in his car. Mrs. Dent acknowledged his courtesy and presently departed.

This was True's first visit to the flat in Finborough Road. He did not leave a good impression behind, for on the following (Sunday) evening Olive Young told her friend Doris Dent that she had no wish to see Major True again. After he had gone she had missed a £5 note from her hand-bag, and she strongly suspected him of taking it. He had shown an admiring interest in her jewellery, too, which she had found extremely unpleasant—and he carried a loaded revolver. He was anxious to meet her again but she did not propose to give him a chance. Olive Young, like Mrs.

Wilson, thought True was not fit for a woman to be alone with. She kept out of his way, and for more than a week True's attempts to see her failed. Realizing presently that the girl was deliberately avoiding him, True tried a new device. Olive Young was on the telephone. He could ring her up, and did so persistently day after day, but still his victim refused to be drawn.

This brings the tale to the end of February, and True's funds were exhausted. This, however, did not prevent him from continuing to drive about town in motor-cars. Much could be done on credit and on worthless cheques. Still, some ready money was necessary. On February 28 True got a few pounds by pawning a gold wristlet watch that did not belong to him. How he came by it is not known, but it is not hard to guess. That evening he and Armstrong visited the Palais de Danse, Hammersmith. There True recognized an ex-flying officer, named Sach, who, like himself, had been employed as a test pilot by the United States War Department in 1917. Sach, though he remembered True as an odd fish, was quite pleased to renew the acquaintance, and invited True and Armstrong to dine with him and his wife on the following evening, which they did. Evidently the proceeds of the gold watch had gone, for he successfully touched Sach for a sovereign.

What followed was characteristic. A few hours after leaving the Sachs—that is, in the small hours of the morning of March 2—True turned up at the Victoria Hotel, Northumberland Avenue. A most annoying thing had happened, he told the night porter. He had been locked out of his flat, having forgotten his latch-key, and had knocked and rung without avail. Could he have a room? The story was a likely enough one. He was given a room. In the morning, having had breakfast at the hotel, he slipped out without paying. An ordinary "bilker" would have got away from that neighbourhood as soon as possible. Not so True. On leaving the Victoria he merely crossed the street and presented himself at the reception bureau of the Grand

Hotel in the capacity of a cross-channel pilot who had just arrived at Croydon that morning from Paris. He wanted a room for a few days, and perhaps the hotel management could arrange to have his luggage fetched up from Croydon the next morning. These matters having been satisfactorily arranged, True's next care was to ring up a West End firm of motor-car proprietors. A chauffeur named Luigi Mazzola took the call. Major True, who was staying at the Grand Hotel, wanted a car at once. Could one be sent immediately? Major True mentioned that he could not pay for the car at the moment, as he had just arrived from Paris by aeroplane and had nothing but French money on him, but he would settle up next day. No objection was made to that, and in the evening Mazzola drove down to the Grand Hotel, picked up his customer, and so became the unwitting actor in the tragedy that was at hand.

That evening True dined with his friend, Armstrong, who was an unmarried man living with his mother. Once again it is to be observed how much more sensitive women were than men to True's abnormality. Mrs. Armstrong was uncomfortable about her son's boon companion. He had visited the house once or twice already, and from what she had seen of him she was certain that he was not quite right in his mind and might even be dangerous. She had spoken to her son about it, but her warning had been disregarded. After dinner Mazzola called with the car and the two men drove off on the usual jaunt—Armstrong blissfully ignorant of the fact that his mother's purse, which contained, *inter alia*, a cheque for £7, was in True's pocket. Nothing noteworthy happened until about eleven o'clock, when True ordered Mazzola to drive to Fulham. He gave Armstrong no reason, and Armstrong, being now accustomed to True's journeyings up and down town, was not interested enough to ask. The car proceeded along the Fulham road until, at the corner of Finborough Road, True ordered the driver to stop. He wanted to look up some friends, he said. Armstrong was to wait for him, he said,

in the car—he would not be long. He got out and dis-
appeared up Finborough Road, but was only away a few
minutes. His friends were not in, he explained, and the car
drove off. It will be observed that although Armstrong did
not know where Olive Young lived he may have met her
in the West End. True knew that he did not know.

On the following evening (March 3) True and Armstrong
were again at the Palais de Danse with Mr. and Mrs. Sach.
In the course of the evening, when Armstrong was not
within hearing, True told the Sachs the tale of "the other
Ronald True," much in the same way as he told Mrs. Wilson
a fortnight before. He even pointed out among the dancers
a man—not in the least resembling him—as the pseudo
Ronald True, who had swindled his mother out of £5,000
by forging cheques and running up bills in his name. He
meant to shoot the other man, he said, and the other man
meant to shoot him. But that was not all. There was another
man, Mr. Sach learned, with whom True was equally if not
more anxious to settle accounts—a man who owed him
money, and who lived *in a basement flat in Fulham*. This
man, like the other, was armed, having a service revolver,
but all the same True was going to go to the flat on Sunday
to kill him. He had been trying to make an appointment
with the man for some days, he said, but so far had failed.
However, he expected to manage it on Sunday. "Look out
for it in the papers on Monday morning," he told Sach. "It
will be one or the other of us." To demonstrate his plan of
operations, True drew a rough plan of Olive Young's flat
on the back of the menu. Sach regarded it all as a tale
"told by an idiot." He thought his eccentric travelling companion of 1917 must be madder than ever. Still, that did
not prevent him from arranging to meet True for lunch the
next day. Having departed from the Sachs, True made his
second expedition to Fulham. The performance of the
preceding night was repeated. At the corner of Finborough
Road the car was stopped. True got out, leaving Armstrong
in the car, and presently came back. Once more his "friends

were not in." I have followed Armstrong's account here, but Mazzola gave a slightly different version. On the Friday night, according to Mazzola, True returned in a minute or two and got Armstrong to accompany him on a second trip along Finborough Road. The two men were absent for several minutes. Armstrong in his evidence said nothing of accompanying True, and the point was not put to him. Mazzola also stated that on either Thursday or Friday, he drove *twice* to Finborough Road. On this point also Armstrong is silent.

The morning of Saturday, March 4, found True penniless. He had Mrs. Armstrong's cheque, of course, and had forged an endorsement, but had had no opportunity of cashing it. This he now expected to be able to do when he met the Sachs for lunch, for, as it conveniently happened, Armstrong was not to be one of the party. About one o'clock he met the Sachs at the Strand Corner House. After lunch, Mrs. Armstrong's cheque was produced. Could Sach oblige him by cashing it, as, this being Saturday, all the banks were shut? Sach was sorry he could not, but ultimately Mrs. Sach managed to cash it at a shop where she was known. Thereupon True paid back the £1 he had borrowed from Sach the previous Wednesday, and the party, driven by Mazzola (who seems to have had a remarkable capacity for giving credit), went off to Richmond to spend a pleasant afternoon. They had tea at the Castle Hotel, where, oddly enough, there happened to be a third person with whom True was at enmity. This, in fact, was an inoffensive stranger who was having tea at a neighbouring table: but True assured the Sachs that he knew the fellow well, having been to school with him at Bedford, that he was a bad man, that he was not treating a girl right, that the girl's name was Olive and she lived in Bedford, and that he (True) had remonstrated with the man about his conduct, though apparently not to the extent of shooting him. Later, after this man had gone, True was called to the telephone—evidently he had asked for a call to be put through—and returned, telling his friends that he had been speaking to "Olive" at Bedford, and also that he had met the man outside again and had spoken to him about his conduct towards the girl. The Sachs could not take this story very seriously: for they had noticed that although True and the supposed miscreant had been in full view of each other, no sign of recognition had passed between them.

The significance of the Richmond incident is this: that True had now told Mr. and Mrs. Sach (1) that there was someone in a basement flat in Fulham from whom he wanted money; (2) that he meant to get that money even if he had to murder someone; (3) that he had been trying, so far without success, to arrange an appointment with the person, but expected to have the critical interview in the basement flat in Fulham on Sunday night; (4) that Monday's papers would certainly announce that murder had been committed in that flat; (5) that he knew a girl called Olive, who was being persecuted by a man; (6) that he had just been telephoning to "Olive."

The party returned to London about nine o'clock. True bade good night to his friends, and ordered Mazzola to drive to the Ring, Blackfriars Road. There he could not help meeting the referee, who naturally took the opportunity of reminding him of his I.O.U. given him on February 17. True had an excuse ready. He had been flying to Bristol, Paris and Marseilles with films of Princess Mary's wedding, and would pay up as soon as he collected the money that was waiting for him at Croydon aerodrome.

Mr. Broadribb, the referee, had to be satisfied with this. True did not wait long at the Ring, but before he left he made a new acquaintance—a Mr. Bishop, who managed bachelor suites in Half Moon Street. He insisted on driving Mr. Bishop home. *En route* they stopped for some refreshment at the Strand Corner House, where True made some inquiries about the rent of apartments which Mr. Bishop was very glad to answer. By the time Mr. Bishop was set down at Half Moon Street, it was eleven o'clock. For the third night in succession—but this time alone—True was driven to Fulham. He got out, as before, at the corner of Finborough Road, saying to Mazzola that he had *urgent business* to see to. As before, he returned, grumbling that he could not find anybody, and drove away.

These midnight visits to Fulham were not True's only attempts to see Olive Young. Throughout that week he had been pestering her with telephone calls trying to arrange a meeting, which the girl steadily refused. Rebuffed in his own name, True tried to pass himself off as Armstrong, but Olive Young recognized the voice and demanded that Armstrong himself should speak. True then tried to make her believe that it was Armstrong's chauffeur that was speaking, but she knew who it was and rang off. The ruse had failed, but the fact that it had been attempted filled Olive Young with alarm. She determined to avoid him more sedulously than ever. Up to Sunday, March 5, she had been quite successful. Mrs. Dent was with her all the afternoon of that day, and in the evening the two women went out to dine together, choosing a place where True was not likely to find them. About half-past ten, somewhat reluctantly, Olive Young parted with her friend at Piccadilly Circus Tube Station. She booked to Earls Court, whence she had a few minutes' walk to Finborough Road. The whole journey would take about half an hour, so she must have been in her flat at about a few minutes to eleven.

Meanwhile True had been up the river, Armstrong having the use of a bungalow at Reading. The pair had spent an idle day, having done nothing more energetic than firing Very lights from a pistol. The attentive Mazzola drove them back to town and late in the evening there was yet another visit to Fulham, arriving about ten minutes past eleven. Everything happened precisely as before. Once more True's friends were not at home. The next thing was to take Armstrong home. On the way Armstrong noticed a tall man running along Fulham Road, and so apparently did True, but no remark was made on it at the time. Armstrong having been got rid of, True once more ordered Mazzola to drive to Fulham. This time there was no stopping at the corner of Finborough Road. The car was to turn into the road and stop at No. 13A. There True got out and descended to the basement flat. Presently True returned. He would not want the car again that night, he said, but Mazzola was to come back for him at Finborough Road at 11 a.m. on the Monday morning. The chauffeur took his orders and departed. True spent the night with Gertrude Yates.

The question naturally arises here why, at the second visit on this fatal night, True did not, as before, stop at the corner of the road, but drove right up to his victim's door. The inference is that on the previous occasions he had merely been reconnoitring and that on his last visit he had ascertained that the opportunity to strike had arrived. A fact elicited at True's trial cleared the whole matter up. Olive Young was in the habit of leaving a light burning in the entrance passage of her flat till she came home, when she used to turn it out; and this light would be visible to anyone who looked down from street level through the fanlight. It is fairly certain that when True drove to the corner of Finborough Road on Thursday, Friday, and Saturday, he ran up to No. 13A, and on each occasion found the light burning in the passage, which meant that his intended victim had not come home yet. But on Sunday night Olive Young arrived home just about eleven o'clock, so that when True peered down from the street a few minutes later he had the satisfaction of observing that the light was out. That was enough. All that remained was to get rid of Armstrong, and then return with all speed to Fulham. There was always the chance, of course, that he might be refused admittance, but that was unlikely. Girls of Olive Young's class cannot afford to make scenes at midnight and appeal to the police on the slightest provocation—particularly when their landlady is not *supposed* to know what their calling is. It is better to take a few risks. And so when

Gertrude Yates found who was knocking at her door, she
bowed to her fate. She let him in, and took her chance.

True's demeanour must have been fairly reassuring, for
at seven o'clock on Monday morning Gertrude Yates was
still peacefully drowsing in her bed, dimly conscious, perhaps, that her companion was up and about at the business
of making early morning tea. This, of course, had to be
done in the kitchen next door, and then True, rummaging
about, found the very thing he wanted in the copper—a
stout rolling-pin. He brought in the tea, and "Olive" sat
up sleepily and took her cup. True slipped round the other
side of the bed. . . .

She gave no trouble. The first blow of the rolling-pin
felled her, sending her cup and saucer crashing to the floor,
and four more were delivered in swift succession. She was
as good as dead, but the murderer was thorough. A towel
thrust deep into her gullet, and the girdle of her dressing-
gown drawn tightly round her neck, finished the job.

True dragged the corpse into the bathroom and left it
lying on the floor. That he should do that and then go to
the trouble of arranging two pillows in the bed to look as
if someone were asleep there, suggests the distorted cunning
of a defective intelligence. Obviously it would have been
far better to have tucked the body in the clothes. True's
action cannot be ascribed to the confusion arising from
haste. The murder was accomplished by half-past seven
and True well knew that the daily servant, Emily Steel, was
not due to arrive before nine o'clock, and would probably
be late. That would give him an hour and a half to lay
hands on anything of value and clear out. The curious thing
is that True, having rifled Gertrude's handbag, which contained £8, and taken the best of the jewellery he could find,
chose to remain in the flat until long after Emily Steel's
arrival. Steel, when she came in, noticed a man's coat in
the sitting-room, but naturally attached no special importance to the fact. She prepared and ate her own breakfast,
and then proceeded to tidy up the sitting-room. Suddenly

a man appeared from the direction of the bedroom. That did not surprise her. She had seen him before. Major True was very affable. "Don't disturb Miss Young," he said, "we were late last night, and she is in deep sleep. I'll send a car round for her at midday." Steel was most obsequious to her mistress's friend, and helped him on with his coat, whereupon he tipped her half a crown, reminding her that he owed her something for getting him a taxi on the last occasion that he had been at the flat. And so he left—two hours after murdering Gertrude Yates. Emily Steel saw him hail a cab at the corner of Finborough Road. A few minutes later she discovered what had happened.

If the slaying of a human being was of small account, there would be something almost ludicrous about True's assurance that his crime could not be brought home to him. For the past fortnight he had been boasting to casual acquaintances that he was going to murder someone, even naming the time and place, though not his victim, which doubtless he regarded as a masterly stroke of cunning, and at the same time he was convinced he could cover up his tracks with the utmost ease. And so it may be imagined that as he was borne along the Fulham Road he reflected with complacency on his morning's work. Olive Young was dead. He had eight pounds odd of her money and the best of her jewellery in his pocket. A few precautions, obvious to a man of his superior intelligence, would completely baffle the police. Meanwhile he must countermand his order to Mazzola to bring the car to Finborough Road; so at the first post office in Fulham Road he stopped the taxi and telephoned to the garage, ordering the car to call first for Mr. Armstrong and then go on to the Strand Corner House. True was next taken with all speed to Coventry Street, Piccadilly Circus, where he stopped at a men's outfitters, telling the taxi to wait. He had dealt at the shop before and was known by the assistants. The first thing he wanted this morning was a *hat*—which, as he did not ordinarily wear one, he no doubt regarded as an astute disguise. Next he

unbuttoned his overcoat and drew the assistant's attention
to some fresh bloodstains. These, he explained, were the
result of a flying accident he had just had, and he thought
he really must have a new suit at once. He was passed on
to the ready-made suits department, where, after trying on
several, he found a lounge suit to his taste. "Not a bad
reach-me-down," he remarked pleasantly. The shop had
always known Major True as a pleasant and jocular gentleman, and this morning he was as affable as ever. While the
assistant was clearing out the pockets of the discarded suit
preparatory to making a parcel of it, he came upon a jewel-
case. True at once opened it, and displayed the rings—
"little mementoes" he had just picked up in France, he
said. A collar and tie completed True's purchases, which
ate up £7 of Olive's cash. His next visit was to a barber
in Wardour Street, where he discharged the cab. At the
barber's he had a shave and brush up, put on his new collar
and tie, and deposited the parcel of bloodstained clothes,
saying he would return for it in a few minutes. There was
one more thing he must do before he met his friend—pawn
the stolen jewellery. He went to a neighbouring pawn-
brokers, redeemed the watch and cigarette-case he had
pledged on the Saturday, and then offered Olive Young's
rings. He wanted £70 for the pair, but had to be content
with £25. Of course, he did not return to the barber's for
his parcel, but hurried off to the rendezvous at Charing
Cross.

Mazzola was waiting with the car when True arrived at
the Corner House. He noted with some surprise (having
regard to the circumstances in which they had parted overnight) that he was wearing a new suit *and a new hat*. True
greeted him with his usual affability, and remarked casually
that he was sorry he had dismissed him the night before as
his stay in the flat had lasted only twenty minutes. A man
and a woman, he said, had got into a violent quarrel, so he
thought it best to leave them to fight it out. Presently he
told the same story to Armstrong. Before he left the Corner

House he encountered Sach, who over the week-end had been worrying a good deal about the cheque transaction to which he had been a party on the Saturday. He did not imagine for a minute that it had been stolen, but for all he knew it might be a "stumer." He explained his fear to True, who at once handed over £7 in notes in case the cheque should be returned. Sach departed much relieved, and True and Armstrong drove off to Hounslow and thence to Feltham, to see some internal-combustion engines in which they were interested. About four o'clock the party were at Croydon, where they had tea and True bought a newspaper. He first asked for the *Sportsman*, and failing to get that asked for the *Star*. Prominent, with big headings, on the front page, was the first news of the murder of Olive Young. True glanced at the paper and then tossed it aside with the remark, "Nothing of interest." The next stop was Richmond, where True must needs buy a new shirt, which he put on there and then. After that they returned to London, dined and drove to the Hammersmith Palace of Varieties, arriving about nine o'clock in time for the "second house." Mazzola was sent back to his garage with instructions to return for them at the end of the show.

Meantime the police had been busy. They had been apprised of the murder of Gertrude Yates within half an hour of True's departure from Finborough Road, and they had not the slightest difficulty in identifying the criminal and picking up his tracks. Some significant information was given to them by ex-Inspector Stockley. Thus it was that when Mazzola returned to his garage in Knightsbridge, he found two Scotland Yard men waiting for him, who, learning where he had left True, ordered him to take them at once to the Hammersmith Palace. Their task was an anxious one. A crowded theatre is an awkward place to make an arrest, particularly when your man is, by all accounts, a homicidal lunatic and carries a loaded revolver. The police were lucky, however, for True and his friend, though they had begun by sitting in the stalls, had exchanged to a box, which enabled the arrest to be made with little delay or disturbance. No one on the stage or in the auditorium had any inkling of the thrilling extra turn that had been going on in one of the boxes. True went quietly.

On being charged True denied all knowledge of the crime. Subsequently he made a statement about seeing, on the Sunday night, a tall man running along the Finborough Road. In due course he was committed for trial, and on May 1 he was brought up at the Central Criminal Court before Mr. Justice McCardie.

III

Prima facie True's crime was prompted by a perfectly sane motive. He needed money. Gertrude Yates had cash and valuables. He murdered her, took everything that was worth taking, lost no time in turning the jewellery into cash, and used every means that suggested itself in his mind to escape detection. That was the sum and substance of the case against True; and the prosecution submitted that it not only did not support, but negatived the suggestion that the murderer of Gertrude Yates was a madman. The view was calculated to appeal to the man in the street, who is also the man in the jury-box, as the obvious common sense of the matter, with the result that True was convicted. Nevertheless it was based on fallacy, viz., that an act that might well be the act of a sane man cannot be the act of an insane one.

Before proceeding to the medical evidence on True's state of mind, let us consider the net result of the facts related above. At the end of 1921 and the beginning of 1922 he had a prolonged fit of apathy and silent brooding. Then, on the vague pretext of business at Bedford, he contrived to leave home and began to lead a vagrant life in the West End of London. He cut himself off from the family and became markedly hostile to his wife. His casual associates in London regarded him as abnormal. Some thought him dangerous, others merely fatuous, but none found him taciturn or apathetic. On the contrary, he was invariably vivacious—the inference being that he was getting plentiful supplies of morphia. Presently he began to commit frauds and thefts. He bought a pistol and ammunition, and talked freely about committing a murder, mentioning first one, then two, and finally three men, with whom he was at deadly enmity, one of them being a man who had an assumed name of Ronald True.

In taking True into custody the police realized that they were dealing with a man who was undoubtedly deranged and probably insane in the full sense of the term. He was at once sent to the prison hospital at Brixton, and practically from the date of his arrest until he was placed in the dock at the Central Criminal Court he was kept under close observation by the medical officer, Dr. East, and his assistant Dr. Young. It was characteristic that he was distinctly popular with his fellow prisoners, being, as always, affable and jocular—but a constant source of trouble and anxiety to the warders and doctors. He slept little, was more or less in an excited state, and, in spite of his jocularity, was easily provoked into violence. One of his first acts was to commit a sudden assault on a fellow prisoner, whom he accused, without any justification, of stealing his food. This incident convinced Dr. East that sedatives were imperative, for there was every indication that if excitement and insomnia were not abated, another murder would be laid to True's account. It is important to observe that the sleeplessness and excitement were not in any way connected with remorse for his crime, or anxiety about his situation; on the contrary, he appeared to be very well pleased with himself, and, while always denying that he had anything to do with the death of Gertrude Yates, he took obvious pleasure in being the central figure of a *cause célèbre*. He was quite facetious about it. One day, shortly after his admission to hospital, he managed to escape to another ward where he knew there was another prisoner charged with murder. This was Henry Jacoby, afterwards hanged for the murder of Lady White. "Here's another for our murderers' club," he shouted. "We only accept those who kill outright"—the same silly pleasantry that he had often exchanged with his friend Armstrong. He was inordinately boastful, incapable of speaking the truth, even when no conceivable purpose could be served by lying, and appeared to have the delusion that people were going about impersonating him. After prolonged observation, Dr. East formed the opinion that True was in a state of congenital mental disorder, aggravated by the morphia habit, and that he was certifiably insane. Dr. Young, the assistant prison doctor, came to the same conclusion. The two doctors reported accordingly.

These opinions were confirmed and in some respects amplified by the eminent alienists, Dr. Percy Smith and Dr. Stoddart, who examined True at the request of his relatives. Their examinations, of course, were separate and independent. Their conclusions were practically identical. To both True boasted about his capacities and achievements, and he seemed elated rather than depressed by his position. There were some signs of confusion and loss of memory. He had well-defined delusions of persecution and the curious stories that he had told Mrs. Wilson and Mr. Sach were repeated to Drs. Smith and Stoddart in considerably greater detail. He carried a revolver, he said, because he had enemies who would shoot him if they got the chance. Among them was a professional gambler, whose name he gave variously as Eaton, Nicholls, or Hobson, who had once "held him up with a gun" because he (True) had pressed him to pay a large sum of money he owed him. Then there was "the other Ronald True," quite a different person who was also "after him with a gun," though why he should persecute him True could not say; all he knew was that people had told him so. Once at Murray's he had caught a glimpse of the "other" and had tried to draw a pistol, but the "other" had slipped out before he could do

so. But this Ronald True was not to be confused with the
other Ronald *Trew* who had been an officer in the army.
According to Dr. Stoddart, True was vague about the identity of his double. He complained that he had been imper-
sonated and persecuted in New York, Brighton, and London,
and seemed to think that he had several persecutors who
all used his name, but he admitted the possibility that there
might only be one who went from place to place after him.

Such being the medical reports it was obvious that True's
defence would be that when the crime was committed he
was insane and not responsible for his actions.

Now when a special defence of insanity is put up, it is
the right of the prosecution to call evidence in rebuttal. As
a rule this presents little difficulty. There are few points
on which doctors will not differ to some degree, and none
that is so provocative of disagreement as the question of a
person's soundness of mind. Further, in considering the
policy to be adopted at the trial the prosecution have regard
to the reports of the prison doctor, and if they decide to
press for a conviction it usually means that they can rely on
the prison doctor to support them in the witness-box. When
this happens the expert testimony given for the prosecution
has a clear advantage in weight over the expert testimony
for the defence; for the latter is called *ad hoc*, whereas the
former is based on observations which may be faulty but
are certainly disinterested. But in the case of True the
reports of the two medical officers of Brixton prison were
adverse to the prosecution. Dr. East, a man of exceptional
experience in the examination of criminal lunatics, and his
assistant, Dr. Young, were emphatic in their opinion that
True was insane, and they concurred in every material
respect with the two distinguished alienists who examined
the prisoner on behalf of the defence. But, notwithstanding
their serious tactical disadvantage, the prosecution decided
to make every effort to secure a conviction. They had True
examined by a fifth medical man, Dr. Cole of St. Mary's
Hospital, an alienist of high standing. Dr. Cole reported

that his own examination did not disclose anything that would justify him in declaring True insane, but his opinion was given subject to a number of important reservations.

Sir Richard Muir, senior Treasury counsel at the Central Criminal Court, who was in charge of the prosecution, was in a dilemma. There was a heavy array of medical evidence against him to which he was unable to raise any effective opposition. If he put Dr. Cole in the box, Dr. Cole's evidence under cross-examination might recoil upon the prosecution with deadly effect. If he did not put Dr. Cole into the box the defence would not fail to enlarge upon the fact that the prosecution with all their resources were unable to produce a single doctor who would swear that True was a sane and responsible man. Sir Richard decided that the latter course was the less dangerous. He did not call Dr. Cole, and relied for achieving his purpose upon cross-examination and the *Rules in M'Naughton's Case*. The event proved the wisdom of his choice. As Dr. Cole was never called his report was never made public. There is reason to believe that he regarded True as mentally deficient rather than insane, inasmuch as that was as far as his own observation would take him, but he was not prepared to traverse the conclusions reached by his professional brethren as the result of their own observations.

To appreciate the meaning of this it is necessary to realize that, for the purpose of bringing down a defence of insanity, the English criminal law thoughtfully provides the prosecution with a double-barrelled gun. First, they can say that the prisoner is not in fact insane. Alternatively, and without prejudice to the first contention, they can submit that, even if the prisoner is in fact insane, his insanity is not of such a nature as to free him from responsibility according to the canons of English law. The two barrels are discharged almost simultaneously, to the great confusion of the jury, who are further confounded by the practice adopted by bar and bench of using the term "insanity" now in the sense of "mental derangement," and now in the

sense of "irresponsibility by reason of mental derangement."
It was to this confusion of the mind of the jury, and still
more in the mind of the public, that most of the heated
controversy over True's case was due. Consequently, it is
worth while to consider for a moment a problem on which
medical men and jurists have expended much time and
breath, ink and paper, but which may be stated with comparative brevity once its true nature has been grasped.

When the law decrees punishment it passes a moral
judgment. It says that the culprit is "responsible," that is
righteously punishable, for what he has done. It is not the
act *per se* that involves the punishment but the wicked state
of mind of which the act is the evidence and fulfilment.
Actus non facit reum nisi mens sit rea. What then con-
stitutes *mens rea*, or wicked mind? Roughly speaking, we
may say that if a person knows what he is doing, he is
righteously punishable for his act. But that is not enough.
The culprit may be fully conscious of the physical nature
and moral quality of his act, but he may have done it
against his will, having been placed under some severe
external compulsion, such as torture and threats of death,
that no man of ordinary courage could be expected to
withstand. In such a case, obviously there is no wicked
mind, for, although he knew what he was doing his mind
did not accompany his act. But even when both volition
and knowledge are present, the law will still sometimes
excuse on the ground of *imperfection of understanding*.
Thus a child of six may well be aware that stealing is
wrong, but if he does steal the law will not punish him,
holding that, despite all appearance of knowledge and
intention, a person of such tender years cannot have enough
"understanding" to have a guilty mind. In the case of
children under seven the law's denial of criminal capacity
is absolute; and even older children, up to the age of
fourteen, will be presumed incapable of *mens rea* until the
contrary be proved.

We have thus three cases in which the moral sense of

the community would not approve of punishment being inflicted on a wrongdoer—(1) when the person did not know what he was doing, as in the case of somnambulism; (2) where the person knew what he was doing, but was overborne by *force majeure*; and (3) where the person suffered from such a defect of "understanding" that it would be unreasonable to impute to him a guilty intention, even although it might be said that, in a sense, he knew and intended what he was doing. If the third category were logically applied, the cause of the defect of understanding would be immaterial. It would apply equally to the child, whose defect is due to immaturity, and to the lunatic, whose defect is due to disease. In point of fact, however, the defect of understanding operates as an excuse only in the case of a child. The law, embodying the traditional psychology of action, which assumes that knowledge necessarily implies control, will not allow it in the case of a lunatic. Indeed, it is doubtful if it would be allowed in the case of a child but for two considerations—first, the fact that everybody knows from immediate experience that the traditional psychology breaks down in the case of a child, and, second, that common humanity, as well as common sense, revolts at the idea of inflicting criminal punishment on a child of tender years—a sentiment which is by no means extended to the adult unsound mind. Consequently, the law will not entertain insanity as an excuse, except where the criminal act comes within the first category; that is to say the accused must show that his alienation of mind was such that he did not know what he was doing, or, if he did know what he was doing, did not know that it was wrong. It is assumed that, if a man does wrong, knowing it to be wrong, he could have refrained from doing it, and that in not refraining he elected to take the consequences. To think otherwise, it is conceived, would be fatal to the administration of the criminal law. Such is the legal doctrine laid down in what are conveniently, but not quite accurately, known as the *Rules in M'Naughton's Case*. These were answers given by the common law judges to a series of questions submitted to them by the House of Lords in the following circumstances:

In the year 1843 much excitement and even alarm was caused by the death, at the hand of an assassin, of Mr. Drummond, private secretary to the Prime Minister, Sir Robert Peel. The murderer was one Daniel M'Naughton, a young Glasgow tradesman of respectable antecedents. The rulers of the country were at that time in a bad state of nerves owing to the prevalence of political agitation, and, when it appeared from M'Naughton's statements that he was under the impression that his victim was the Prime Minister himself, the murder was interpreted as the act of a dangerous revolutionary—and certain colour was lent to the belief by the circumstance that M'Naughton came from Glasgow, which was then, as now, regarded as a revolutionary plague-spot. But when the wretched M'Naughton was brought to trial at the Central Criminal Court, it abundantly appeared that he was far advanced in what is now known as paranoia, a form of insanity, progressive and apparently incurable, and characterized by systematized delusions of persecution. The only ground for giving a political complexion to his crime was his expressed belief that his insatiable and invisible persecutors were the "Tories" and "Jesuits." The evidence was so plain that the presiding judges (Tindal, C. J., Williams, J., and Coleridge, J.) stopped the case and directed the jury to find a verdict of *Not guilty on the ground of insanity*, which being done, M'Naughton was ordered to be detained in Bethlem Hospital.

The result of the trial created even more indignation in high quarters than the crime itself. Queen Victoria herself was particularly incensed. Her correspondence with her Ministers on the subject makes curious reading. There is an excuse for the young Queen in that she herself shortly before had been the subject of a feeble attempt by the demented youth Oxford, who, like M'Naughton, was acquitted. The House of Lords, on the initiative of Brougham, gravely debated the question, and it was decided to ask Her Majesty's judges to declare to what extent the law of England allowed unsoundness of mind as an answer to a criminal charge. To that end their lordships formulated a series of hypothetical questions, to which the judges (Maule, J., dissenting) gave the answers that have come to be known as the *Rules in M'Naughton's Case*. The substance of the Rules has already been indicated, viz., that insanity is no answer to a criminal charge, unless it amounts to such a disorder of mind that the accused did not know the nature and quality of his act, or, if he did know the nature and quality of his act, did not know that it was wrong.

Whether this was an accurate statement of the law as previously administered may well be doubted. Hitherto insanity had been a comparatively rare defence, being put forward only in cases where it was impossible to ignore it; and the law's attitude had never been clearly defined. Everything depended on the prepossessions of the judge who happened to try the particular case. Some judges took the "wild beast" view, viz., that insanity was no excuse unless it amounted to a fury in which the accused had no appreciation of objective fact. Others were content to direct that if a man were manifestly out of his senses at the time of the act, he should be held guiltless. The latter was the more humane and sensible view, though in practice it was very sparingly applied. Judges and juries regarded the defence of insanity with great suspicion, believing—with some justification in an age in which the phenomena of mental disorder had never been scientifically studied—that unsoundness of mind could easily be simulated. This belief is still widely entertained (as the newspaper correspondence upon True's case showed) though nowadays, as a matter of fact, of all forms of malingering feigned insanity is the easiest to detect. On the whole, it may be fairly said that prior to 1843 the question of an insane prisoner's responsibility was left to the jury as an issue of pure fact to be determined by evidence alone and not with reference to any special rules of law. The answers of the judges changed all that. Not that that was their intention. Far from it. All the judges had in mind was to state the conditions which, in their mind, would justify a jury in inferring irresponsibility. Following the psychological conceptions that were then prevalent, they doubtless conceived that where these conditions were not satisfied, there could be no evidence on which a jury could find that a prisoner was not responsible for his actions. At the same time, the answers, being limited to the terms of the questions, could not properly claim to be exhaustive.

The answers served an immediate purpose of some value. Their tenor was sufficiently reassuring to put an end to the monstrous demand—seriously advanced by respectable and eminent persons—that insanity should in no circumstances be accepted as an excuse for crime, and that lunatics should be punished in the same manner as sane offenders. No more was heard of that proposal. But the ultimate effect of the answers was unfortunate. As an eminent judge once remarked, they are so drafted that on strict interpretation hardly anyone is ever mad enough to come within them, yet the three judges who concurred in directing M'Naughton's acquittal also concurred in the answers, though certainly Daniel M'Naughton would not have come within them. The inference is obvious. The judges never intended that their answers should be elevated to the status of rules of law, exhaustive and requiring strict interpretation. That, however, is what they have become. Mr. Justice Maule, who dissented from his brethren, foresaw the danger. He returned his answers more or less under protest, pointing out that the principles of English Law were to be extracted from the judicial decisions upon specific cases after argument by counsel, and that answers given to abstract questions without aid of argument might prove embarrassing to the administration of justice.

The embarrassment exists, but thanks to the common sense which, on the whole, animates the administration of English Law, it is less serious than one might suppose. Where the prisoner is a manifest lunatic, he is usually dealt with upon arraignment, being found unfit to plead to the indictment, whereby the necessity for a nice inquiry into his knowledge of the nature and quality of his act is avoided. Where the prisoner is a certified lunatic, who has killed or maimed an asylum attendant, judges have sometimes refused to proceed to trial, in spite of the fact that as a rule the M'Naughton test would require such a culprit to be held fully responsible for his act. Difficulty arises only when the prisoner is allowed to plead and issue is joined on the special defence that he is insane or was insane at the date of the act *and was not responsible*. It is important to remember these last words. They mean that proof of mental disorder, though essential, is not enough to establish the defence. The mental disorder must be of such a kind as to satisfy the conditions laid down by the M'Naughton Rules. Similarly, the prosecution, in tendering rebutting evidence, is not required to prove that the man is sane, but only that his mental condition satisfies the test of legal responsibility. In practice, however, the prosecution prefers to fight the case on the broad question of fact, viz., the existence of grave mental disorder, for no jury will convict a man whom they believe to be mad simply in obedience to a lawyer's canon. As a rule the accused's mental condition is sufficiently obscure to allow this course to be taken. If the defence submits medical and other evidence of insanity, the prosecution may, in like manner, produce rebutting evidence; and in directing the jury the judge will invoke the M'Naughton Rules as a ready means of resolving conflict.

To this device, however, there are serious objections. In the first place, it pretends to distinguish, by an infallible rule, those lunatics who are morally guilty from those who are not—a claim that implies an extraordinary, indeed superhuman knowledge. Secondly, it is extremely confusing to the plain citizens in the jury-box, who hold the sensible view that if a man is mad he cannot be responsible, and conversely that if he is responsible he cannot be mad. Consequently, when the judge tells them that the medical evidence is insufficient to prove that the prisoner was not responsible for his act, they take it as a direction that he is not mad, and that the doctors called for the defence have merely been putting up an academic case on behalf of a rascal, who for all practical purposes is as sane as anybody in Court.

True's was not the ordinary case, however. There was no conflict to be resolved. The medical evidence as to his insanity was uncontroverted, cogent, and conclusive. But Sir Richard Muir had no difficulty in showing that it did not satisfy the conditions prescribed by the M'Naughton Rules. In cross-examination, argument, and speech he pressed his point with the utmost skill and pertinacity. Had the temper of the jury been different, this insistence would have been useless. But as the case proceeded it became clear that the facts that to the medical men were so eloquent of profound mental disorder, would convey to the jury only the picture of a depraved callous monster, who, being in need of ready cash, thought to raise a few pounds by murdering and robbing a defenceless woman.

Sir Henry Curtis Bennett fully realized all this. He was aware of the fact that, although he had all the evidence on his side, it would be insufficient to counterbalance the jury's will to convict unless it were supplemented by a strong direction from the judge. Accordingly his main effort was to get such a direction. The difficulty was the M'Naughton Rules. In a long legal argument Sir Henry submitted that the Rules ought to be strictly interpreted inasmuch as they had been considerably relaxed by judicial interpretation, particularly during recent years. Mr. Justice M'Cardie, who always enjoyed debating a novel point, entered sympathetically into the argument, but the desired direction was not forthcoming. And so in the end Sir Richard's argument prevailed, not so much by its logic as by its congruence with the jury's reluctance to believe that they had to deal with a lunatic. The doctors might say he was mad, but the jury did not believe them. On May 5, after a trial lasting five days, True was found *Guilty* and sentenced to death.

That there should be an appeal against the verdict was inevitable in view of the strength and unanimity of the medical evidence. On May 25 the case came before the Court of Criminal Appeal, consisting of the Lord Chief Justice (Lord Hewart), Mr. Justice Greer, and Mr. Justice Acton. The ground of the appeal was that Mr. Justice M'Cardie had misdirected the jury on the law as to the criminal responsibility of the insane. Sir Henry Curtis Bennett argued, as he had argued at the trial, that the Rules of the M'Naughton Case, if not superseded, had at least been considerably modified by eighty years of judicial inter- pretation; and he submitted that these modifications had not been given sufficient weight in the judge's summing up. Regarded from a strictly legal standpoint, his case was hopeless from the beginning. There was no reported case of the M'Naughton Rules being used to test if an *admitted* lunatic was responsible for his act. This seems strange, seeing that that was the precise point to which the M'Naughton Rules were directed; but it is so. In practice, we have seen, the Rules have only been applied where the prosecution was prepared to contest the allegation of insanity on its merits, and where there was at least *some* evidence on which a jury could find that the accused was not insane in any reasonable sense of the word. They have been maintained, not for their ostensible purpose of deter- mining the responsibility of an insane person, but as a handy rule of thumb whereby in view of a conflict of evi- dence, a jury could decide whether a person was in fact insane. The effect of this has been that, in so far as the Rules have received judicial discussion, it has always been in circumstances favourable to their maintenance. It is true that there are many judicial *dicta* that are not in harmony with the Rules; but, as Sir Richard Muir, replying to Sir Henry Curtis Bennett, was able to show, they are mostly *obiter*, and in any case have never received countenance from the Court of Criminal Appeal. True's appeal, then, had little support from the authorities. Its substantial ground was that the Court of Criminal Appeal, recoiling from the proposition that an undisputed lunatic was responsible for his acts, might be induced to review the M'Naughton Rules in the light of modern knowledge and to re-state the English Law as to the criminal responsibility of the insane.

Such a hope, however, implied a more comprehensive view of its function than the Court of Criminal Appeal has ever been disposed to take. Rightly or wrongly that Court has always been timorous of judicial adventures; and in the case of a murderer's appeal on the ground of insanity its attitude has always been defined with reference to two questions: (1) What is the law as laid down in the M'Naughton Rules? and (2) Was there evidence on which the jury could return a verdict in accordance with the law? In True's case the answers to these questions were necessarily adverse, inasmuch as, despite the unanimous opinion of the doctors that he was insane, there was substantial evidence that he knew what he was doing and that it was wrong. The Court accordingly, without the least hesitation, dismissed the appeal, and so far from discussing and modifying the *Rules in M'Naughton's Case*, explicitly reaffirmed them in their entirety as the law of the land. As to the objection that it was contrary to the public conscience that a lunatic should suffer the death penalty, the Court accepted the view presented by counsel for the Crown that it was unnecessary to consider that point, as it could be dealt with more conveniently by the Home Secretary. In taking this course the Court merely followed its own precedents, but it is a question whether the circumstances of True's case did not call for a departure from a practice the soundness of which is not free from doubt. According to the ancient maxim, it is the duty of a court to prefer a wide to a narrow view of its jurisdiction. *A fortiori*, when its jurisdiction is undoubted, it ought not to refrain from dealing with a difficult general problem simply because substantial justice in the particular case can be secured through executive action. Such an attitude is open to the objection not only of impairing the authority of the Court, but of thrusting upon the Executive a responsibility that it ought not to be called upon to bear.

IV

It will be convenient at this point to sum up the position as it now stood. At True's trial there was evidence, uncontroverted and incontrovertible, that he was insane; nevertheless the jury found him *Guilty*. They were justified in doing so by the fact that by the law of England insanity does not necessarily imply irresponsibility. But even if the law had been different, and the jury had been directed that insanity *simpliciter* was a good defence, it is tolerably certain that their verdict would still have been Guilty. In that case, of course, the Court of Criminal Appeal would probably have been obliged to set the verdict aside. But, the law being as it is, the Court of Criminal Appeal saw no ground for interfering with the jury's findings, and turned over further action, if any, to the Secretary of State. This brings us to the point at which True's case ceased to be merely an Old Bailey sensation and became the occasion of a furious gust of public passion that for the moment threatened to sweep the Home Secretary out of office and even compromised the existence of a ministry that could ill afford to take unpopular courses even in minor matters.

The Criminal Law of England contains a very notable anomaly. It lays down that even a lunatic may, in certain conditions, be held responsible for his act, but it also lays down that if the act be one that involves the judgment of death, judgment is not to be executed so long as he remains a lunatic. The reasons for the latter rule are variously given by the old writers. One says it is because a lunatic, by reason of his lunacy, might be unable to allege some valid bar to execution, and another is because it is against the conscience to execute judgment of death upon a person who is not in a condition to make his peace with God. These reasons are purely speculative, and in effect mean no more than that, for whatever reason, the public conscience recoils from the idea of punishing the insane with death. The rule is far older than the *Rules of the M'Naughton Case*—Coke speaks of it as being well settled law in his time—but no attempt has been made to define the kind or degree of insanity that entitles an insane person to its benefit. It is enough that he should be insane. The rule presents some curious results. Thus a man, who, being sane, commits a murder and is duly sentenced to death, must be respited if he becomes insane while awaiting execution. On the other hand an insane murderer whose insanity is not of the kind to satisfy the M'Naughton Rules, and who, while awaiting trial or execution, recovers his sanity will be hung for it. But such rapid changes of mental condition are uncommon. The murderer who is found to be mad while under sentence was in all probability mad at the time of his crime, and *vice versa*. It may very well happen, therefore, that the same facts that are unavailing to prevent a prisoner's condemnation will effectually prevent his punishment. In such a case the law in theory says to the culprit—"Your insanity is no excuse for your crime. But we do not like the idea of hanging a madman, so we propose to wait till you recover your reason, in which case you will duly suffer the punishment that the law has justly decreed for the abominable thing you did when you were mad." That is the theory. The practice is somewhat different. Once granted, a respite on the ground of insanity is never withdrawn. The public conscience once more cannot stomach the monstrous logic of the law. The death sentence is not commuted; it is simply not executed. Meantime the prisoner is removed to Broad-

moor to remain there for the rest of his life precisely as if
the defence of insanity had succeeded. It is important to
understand these matters in view of their bearing upon the
last and most notorious phase of the True case.

As the evidence of True's crime was unfolded at the trial,
it became obvious to every lawyer that followed it that so
far as True was personally concerned it was a matter of
indifference what verdict the jury chose to return, and that
when the case for the defence had been closed an insurance
company would have been justified in covering the ultimate
risk of his neck at a nominal premium. Immediately after
the trial, Mr. Justice M'Cardie, as was his bounden duty,
drew the Home Secretary's attention to the nature of the
medical evidence that had been given, and as soon as True's
appeal had been disposed of the Home Secretary took the
action prescribed in such a case by Section 2 (4) of the
Criminal Lunatics Acts, 1884. He appointed a commission
of three medical men to examine True and report on his
state of mind. The medical men were Sir Maurice Craig,
lecturer on mental diseases at Guy's Hospital; Dr. Dyer,
medical member of the Prisons Commission; and Sir John
Baker, formerly medical superintendent of Broadmoor.
They saw the condemned man, and found what the medical
men who gave evidence at the trial had found—an undoubted lunatic. In view of their unanimous report the
Home Secretary had no option but to respite the execution
and order True's removal to Broadmoor, and public intima-
tion of the fact was given in the usual way.

A Home Secretary's lot is not a happy one. His duties
are often disagreeable, and many discretions are vested in
him of such a thankless nature that he counts himself lucky
if he can exercise a majority of them without incurring
odium. An error of judgment may entail unpopularity and
even resignation, but that is all in a day's work. What he
has the right to expect is that he shall not be blamed for
simply obeying the law. Mr. Secretary Shortt had no choice
as to his course of action in the True case. None the less

he had to face a tornado of execration from the Press and
the public.

To understand the uproar that ensued upon the respite
of True it must be remembered that only a day or so before
True's respite was announced, Henry Jacoby, the youth
whom True had encountered so facetiously in the Brixton
Prison Hospital, had been allowed to go to the scaffold in
spite of a strong recommendation to mercy by the jury that
convicted him. The circumstances of Jacoby's crime were
abominable—hardly less so than True's—but owing to his
youth popular sentiment favoured a reprieve. Accordingly,
when it appeared that Jacoby having died True was to live,
the Metropolitan Press, from the highest to the lowest, fell
into a paroxysm of fury. The Home Secretary's head on a
charger was demanded in leading articles in which ignorance
of the law was equalled, if not surpassed, by disregard of
facts. The correspondence columns were flooded with angry
protest. The miserable Jacoby was invested with a martyr's
halo. He was more sinned against than sinning, but he was
only a working man's son and he had killed a knight's
widow and therefore had to hang; while a moral monster
like True, who happened to be well-connected, and whose
victim was only a poor outcast, was sent off to enjoy the
amenities with which life at Broadmoor was supposed to
be surrounded. Things that could only be hinted at in print
were stated and believed in every suburban railway carriage
and public-house. True was the illegitimate son of Lady
"This" or Lady "That"—various names were mentioned
with full assurance—who by the potent social influences
she could muster had induced the Home Secretary to enter
into a flagitious conspiracy with the doctors to save her
son's neck. The very Constitution was declared to be in
danger. What was the use of a jury saying a man was not
insane if the Home Secretary could set aside their verdict?
The Courts of Law had been flouted, and trial by jury was
being superseded by trial by "Harley Street." Even distinguished lawyers moved by professional prejudice and the

general outcry were inclined to think that there was something in this last alarm, and wrote letters to *The Times* about it. The pundits of psychological medicine retorted sharply, and the secular feud between the two professions broke out again over the M'Naughton Rules with unprecedented fury. Plenty of sparks flew, but there was not much illumination.

Of course, the Home Secretary was called upon to explain his action in the House of Commons. Members vied with each other in putting down questions on the "True Scandal," and the general opinion was that Mr. Shortt would be humiliated to the dust. He wasn't. He read the House a stiff but lucid lecture on the law of England with respect to insane criminals. When he rose the House was actively hostile. Before he had finished members began to think the least said about True the better, and when he sat down, with that quick generosity and shrewd appreciation of plain facts that characterize the House of Commons, they cheered him heartily. After that not much could be said. The popular Press, having committed itself deeply, had to make the best retreat it could think of. A continuance of the hue and cry against the Minister was impossible and there were some grumblings about the necessity of amending the law, and a half-hearted attempt was made to represent the medical profession as the real villains of the piece. It was suggested that they had a design to undermine the fabric of criminal justice by means of the pernicious doctrine that all criminals were insane. But Mr. Shortt's statement had knocked the life out of the agitation, and within a few days the London public had found something else to think about.

The outburst of popular passion was ugly and discreditable, but it was excusable enough. Nobody realized or could be expected to realize the fantastic complexity of the English law as to the criminal lunatic. In the first place the issue decided by the Courts was misapprehended. It was thought that the substantial question of True's alleged insanity had been dealt with and that further inquiry had been precluded. It completely mystifies the plain man when he is told that the Criminal Courts are not concerned to find out whether a man is sane or insane, but only if he is "responsible in Law." To this confusion another was presently added. By a false analogy with the general exercise of the prerogative of mercy, it was assumed that the Home Secretary had a discretion and that he had gone out of his way to order an inquiry into True's mental condition. Why had he not ordered an inquiry into Jacoby's case? In fact, the Home Secretary has no discretion. If he has information suggesting that a prisoner under sentence of death is insane, he is obliged by the Criminal Lunatics Act, 1884, to order an inquiry. In Jacoby's case he had no such information. On the contrary all the information he had was all the other way. No suggestion that Jacoby was insane had been put forward at the trial or at any other time. But in True's case both the trial Judge and the Court of Criminal Appeal had directed attention to the prisoner's mental condition, and even if the judges had been silent it would have been impossible for the Home Secretary and his legal advisers to ignore the evidence given at the trial, especially the evidence given by the prison doctors. That so far Mr. Shortt had no choice the better informed of critics had been willing to allow, but it was said that the Criminal Lunatics Act did not require him to take any action on the doctors' report. This contention, which was seriously urged, even by lawyers, was based on a complete misunderstanding of the scope and purpose of the statute. It is not the Criminal Lunatics Act, but the Common Law, that ordains that an insane prisoner must be respited. All that the statute does is to prescribe a procedure for ascertaining if a prisoner is insane, and for dealing with him if he is so found. It in no way cuts down the Common Law doctrine—indeed, it presupposes it by making specially stringent provision for the examination of prisoners under sentence of death. The confusion was due to the fact that the statute does not allow the Secretary of State a discretion as to the removal of the prisoner to an establishment for the insane; for, if the prisoner's sentence is due to expire at no distant date and his condition permits, it may be more convenient simply to keep him in the prison hospital; but obviously such a course would be inappropriate in the case of a prisoner under sentence of death. He must be removed.

Such is the history of True's case, which is unique in the clearness with which it displays the welter of paradox into which the English law has fallen in attempting to find a solution of the difficulty of the criminal lunatic. The difficulty is likely to become more acute, and the inadequacy of the English solution—if it can be so described—still more evident with every advance in our knowledge of mental disorders. The English law is defended on the ground that, for all its illogicality, it has worked well, and that in practice no substantial injustice is done. There is a good deal of truth in this though it is not the whole truth. As we have seen, the M'Naughton Rules have been maintained in being by the judicious conduct of the Crown in never pressing for a conviction on technical grounds where they are unable seriously to dispute that the prisoner is, in the ordinary sense of the word, insane. In True's case that sound rule was not observed. Sir Richard Muir, who doubtless had his reasons, evidently thought it important that the principle that a lunatic may be responsible to the criminal law should be affirmed even if it was barren of practical consequences. He had his way, with what result we have seen.